Early Settlers in Ontario, Canada

Early Settlers in Ontario, Canada

The Hogg, Ramsay, and Breimer Families

by Wilhelmine Ramsay Hogg Sias

Peggy Sias Lantz, Editor

Woodsmere Press, LLC
Pendleton, South Carolina

EARLY SETTLERS IN ONTARIO, CANADA:

THE HOGG, RAMSAY, AND BREIMER FAMILIES

Copyright, 1981, Peggy Sias Lantz

With additional material added, 2014

Woodsmere Press, LLC
P.O. Box 726
Pendleton, South Carolina 29670
www.woodsmerepress.com
www.peggysiaslantz.com

LIBRARY OF CONGRESS CONTROL NUMBER: 2014959049

PUBLISHER'S CATALOG-IN-PUBLICATION DATA

Sias, Wilhelmine Ramsay Hogg.

Early Settlers in Ontario, Canada: The Hogg, Ramsay, and Breimer Families / by Wilhelmine Ramsay Hogg Sias / Peggy Sias Lantz, Editor / 2nd ed.

Pendleton, SC. Woodsmere Press. © 2014.

viii, 183 p. cm.

Includes Index and Name Index

1. History. 2. Emigration. 2. Hogg. 3. Ramsay. 4. Breimer. 5. Ontario. 6. Canada. I. Lantz, Peggy Sias. II. Title.

ISBN-13 978-0-9679600-9-8 (5.5 x 8.5 in., paperback)

Printed in the United States of America

This book is given with love

to all the members of their family.

Peggy Sias Lantz, her granddaughter

and

Fred R. Sias, Jr., her grandson and book designer.

Contents

Contents

Contents

Billie's Soliloquy

I am 65.

I was born in 1873 and this is 1938,

Which makes me 65,

Doesn't it?

I do not mind the years;

They have been kind to me,

Giving me health, vitality, and the joy of living,

In spite of all the hard knocks,

The ups and downs, and the reverses.

I out-work, out-walk, out-play

Most of my younger friends,

And cannot see that my ambition is less,

Though it has changed.

I can hold my head up proudly,

And say to all the world

"I am 65."

And I do,

Though all the world seems determined

To break down my morale,

Crush my spirit,

And make me a poor, dependent, old lady,
Not worthy of life,
But suffered to live on
Because, of course,
We are civilized people.

Much is said these days
About pensions for the aged –
Such a depressing word, "aged" –
But it is stressed.
Our young literati,
And even older scholars,
Come out with statements
Of the uselessness and even detriment
Of persons over even 40.
Young people,
You'll soon be there.
Time passes so quickly.
Beware of what you say,
For one of these mornings you will wake up
And realize that you are classed
With the derelicts.

The old ladies themselves
Groan and sigh and say,
"It's my age, I guess,"
"We're growing old,"

"Can't expect to be well and lively at my
   age,"
Blaming it on the years,
When it is wrong living
And thinking
That brings old age at 65.

They are all as a rule
Very kind and patronizing,
Planning to take care of us
In herds,
And paying out doles
To the worthy and needy
After a thorough investigation.

I don't want to be investigated.
I don't want to be taken care of.
All I want is a chance to earn a modest liv-
   ing
And be useful in my community
Until I am really old.

With this thought, Wilhelmine Ramsay Hogg Sias set out to chronicle what she knew and remembered of her family's history and background, her childhood, her training as a nurse in Chicago, her marriage, and her early days in Florida.

The Name "Hogg"

The origin of the name Hogg is uncertain. The Ettrick Shepherd claimed a Norwegian origin. According to Ferguson's Etymology, the history of the family extends back into the centuries, the name Hog being of Gothic origin and said to mean "violent warrior".

The oldest reference to the name Hoge is in 1425 when Patrick Hoge and Gilbert Hoge, Squires, are named among the gentlemen who "debydit the marches betwixt Ridbath and Remersyde". Sir Andrew Haig, Laird of Remersyde, had been the first to drop the spelling "de Haga". The names are all the same, being in the same neighborhood, and suggest the probability that they all descended from Petrus de Haga who came from Normandy in 1150.

The meaning of the word in North America has caused bearers of the name no end of embarrassment and chagrin. The joke seems irresistible and is expressed freely on all occasions — and by people seldom guilty of an offense of that kind — so that we have had to harden ourselves to it and build up a defense of nonchalance. Or else change the spelling, which has been done in many instances.

The Scottish pronunciation, with long "o", isn't used in this country and seems an affectation, but it is really the proper way to pronounce it.

It seems a shame to spoil a good name in such a silly way.

If you look in a genealogy, you will find quite a list

of variations on the Hogg name, a few famous. They all seem to be farmers of some kind, or writers and newspapermen — dreamers and poets with little real business inclination. The "gentleman farmer's life" combined with literary pursuits seems to be the ideal attainment in this world. The only trouble with it is that it is expensive, and money has to be made to keep it running smoothly, and making money cuts into one's time!

The Hogg Family in Scotland

I did not become interested in the early history and connections of my family until after my father and nearly every other member of his family had gone on to another world. Suddenly I wanted to know all about them and wrote to the few remaining cousins. They knew almost as little as I did, although they had lived all their lives in the same little town, where Great-grandfather Hogg and his associates built their small homes in 1829.

Mr. Young has written a book about the beautiful little city of Galt, Ontario, and in it I found answers to a few of my questions. The biography of James Hogg, the Ettrick Shepherd, by Sir George Douglas, answered a few more.

My hope of going to Scotland and Canada to look up the original records has not been realized — too many wars and depressions, so what I write is a mere outline. Our children at present are not especially interested, but a time will come when at least one of them will be — and for that one I write.

My Great-grandfather Francis Hogg, was born in Selkirkshire, Scotland.

Of their life in Scotland I know nothing definite, but knowing the locality — Selkirkshire, Scotland — and reading the life of James H. Hogg and others, one can imagine. Selkirkshire, formerly known as "Ettrick Forest", is an inland county, hilly and affording good pasture. Large numbers of sheep are raised, Sheviot breed prevailing, and running through the area is the Tweed River and its tributaries, "Ettrick" and "Yarrow". The town, Selkirk, is about 40 miles south-southeast of Edinburgh.

In Scotland, though occupying a modest grade in the social scale, the Hoggs were of old and respectable family (an old-fashioned way of expressing it). They are said to have claimed descent from Haug, a more or less mythic Viking. There was a marked Scandinavian element among them. Many a shepherd lad might have been seen in 1880 with features, hair, and frame of the typical Scandinavian. The name came from Haug or Haig of the Northern tongue. Their lineage, according to Sir George Douglas, was a thing to be proud of, for beyond dispute they sprang from peasants of sound physical constitution and honorable life.

Their home in Scotland was among the rounded grassy hills of Selkirkshire, and they were shepherds. Anciently, it was known as Ettrick Forest, the hunting ground of Scottish kings.

In 1880, the entire county had a population of only 5,388. There were no roads, except the fairly good one to Selkirk town, and even that one was so bad that it required four hours to travel the sixteen miles in time of snow. Often they had no communication to the outside world for months. In September, 1899, the date of the publication of Douglas' book, he says, "All this is altered now."

Great-grandfather Hogg must have been a few years younger than the Ettrick Shepherd, who was born in 1770 and may have been the son of one of his three brothers. The Ettrick Shepherd was said to be an uncle in our family, and we had a violin at home that was said to be his, but they were all very vague about relationships, and too busy earning a living to think

7

or do anything about it. And, unfortunately, when I could have found the answers to my questions, I was not much interested.

The Hogg Family in Galt, Ontario

The roots of my family are deep in the "old country". My grandfathers and grandmothers were all born across the ocean, and came to Canada in its pioneer days. The Hoggs of Selkirkshire, Scotland, came in 1829; the Ramsays from the Mull of Cantire, Scotland, a little later; and the Breimers of Hesse-Darmstadt, Germany, in 1852 or '53. They were all among the early settlers of Ontario: The Hoggs and Ramsays in what is now the lovely little town of Galt, and the Breimers in Waterloo, not more than ten miles away, in the center of one of the richest agricultural districts of the Province.

Great-grandfather Francis Hogg and his family, including two sons, James, the oldest, and a younger son named George, sailed with other families in the "Argus" of Workington, England, in June of the year 1829, for the New World. The voyage took nine weeks and two days, and they were bound for Galt, Ontario, Canada.

In 1829, when he landed in Canada, Great-grandfather Francis had at least two sons. James, the older of the two, must have been between 14 and 16. James' son Francis was born in 1845 and was their second child, so I figure that Great-grandfather Francis was born in the 1790s.

Where they lived in the town, how many there were

in the family, and how they prospered is unknown to me. Mr. Young mentions Francis and his son, James, in his book, in connection with the library. They no doubt took part in all the activity of the community and got along as well as the average.

James was rather tall and large, blue-eyed and sandy-haired, with whiskers when I knew him — the Scandinavian type claimed by the Ettrick Shepherd, but without his talent and force of character. He was strong and healthy, and no doubt did a lot of the hardest kind of work, clearing the land of timber and stones and plowing it for the wheat crop. He was too fond of the outdoors and fishing and hunting to be much of a student, but like all the family, he leaned toward books and culture, and — with his father — was active in promoting the first library and erecting a schoolhouse or church.

He was a jolly companionable person, who loved to sit around the tavern drinking whiskey and joking with his friends. The tavern was the only meeting place for the men, and the "flowing bowl" went round. Scotch whiskey from the local distillery sold for 20 cents a quart, and like most of the men, he drank too much.

He married bonny Barbara Ramsay, and they must have been a good-looking couple and much in love. She must have soon found out that she had married a playboy who could not be depended upon to care for his farm and his family.

James did work heartily at times (especially at a "bee", no doubt), but I guess he could not be depended upon to carry it through, and poor little Barbara, with the children coming at regular intervals until there were eight, had the responsibility on her own shoulders. It is no wonder if she became bitter and complaining. Being the oldest son, he should have inherited his father's estate, but when Francis died, he left it all to George, the younger son.

Uncle Geordie was a quiet, nice-looking elderly gentleman when I saw him, living in a pleasant little house surrounded by lawn and trees with his wife and children. We were there for "tea", and it was all very comfortable and attractive. He was entirely different from his brother, James, in disposition and appearance — quiet, retiring, and reliable. He naturally did not take to the life and things James enjoyed so much.

George had at least two children, Jessie and Jack, and the daughter, Jessie, later was Mrs. Jack V. Scott. She was there the day I called, but was unmarried at that time. Mrs. Hogg was there, too, but I do not remember her at all. I saw Jessie again when she was Mrs. Scott in Parry Sound and liked her very much.

These two sons of Francis Hogg lived the rest of their lives and died in Galt.

James' oldest child was a daughter, Christine, who married early and died when her first child was born.

Frank (my father), who came next, talked often of his sister, whom he admired so much and loved to watch at her sewing. The click of a needle always reminded him of her. Father was the main support of the family at twelve. He not only had to earn money, but he had to go to the tavern and bring his father home. It is no wonder he was a strict teetotaler and hated to see us drink anything out of a glass except milk and water.

He finally managed to get a small sawmill on the river, in which his father worked also, and a small cottage on South Water Street near the mill. There Mother went as a bride, and there, two years after, I was born.

Father's sister, Maggie, was born third. She married William Ira Anderson and lived on a farm near Galt. They had three sons: William Jr., Brock, and Archie, all departed.

James followed. When he was a man and on his way to Manitoba, he stopped in Parry Sound to see us. I like him very much. He married Aunt Martha in a year or two, and they have the finest family of boys and girls — eight or nine of them. He seems to have prospered in every way. Mother paid them a short visit on her way home from the West. Uncle Jim had died, but Aunt Martha and their many children and grandchildren were all there, owning fine farms around the neighborhood. Mother liked Aunt Martha so much and corresponded with her regularly.

Then there was Archibald, who became a brakeman on the Credit Valley Railroad, and was knocked off the top of the train by something while it was crossing a high bridge and was hurled to the valley below. He was quite young.

Aunt Charlotte married Uncle Peter Campbell and they moved to Forest, Ontario, where Uncle Pete had a book store and played in the band. They had a cute little home and some very nice friends. I spent a month with them when I was 18. Auntie was nice-looking and dressed well. They both sang in the choir, and seemed very prosperous and happy to me. They had no children.

Edward was the youngest. He had dark curly hair and blue eyes — a good-looking boy. I was there at the old home one Sunday when I was only four years old, and he brought a girl friend home for the day. After dinner they sat out under the tall fir trees and sang "Pull for the Shore, Sailor, Pull for the Shore" and other well-known hymns. Not long after that he disappeared and has never been definitely heard of since. Grandma grieved over it the rest of her days. When I saw her the last time, she was still trying to figure out the reason: Was she to blame? Had she done this or neglected to do that? How he could have done it to her, I cannot understand.

Grampa Jamie and Grandma Barbara

When I knew Grandfather James, he was "poor", living on a little farm on the outskirts of Galt. Grampa Jamie and Grandma Barbara lived there to the end of their days. There was a small orchard, garden, and some grain fields surrounded by stone fences. I can imagine how my father and his brothers worked gathering all those stones and hauling them to place. The pastures are still littered with them. The soil was rich and produced the finest oats and wheat. When I think of Galt, I smell wheat.

The house was small and unadorned, but always had an air of comfort and refinement, for which dear Grandmother deserves all the credit. Around it grew tall fir trees, their branches spreading out at least 40 or 50 feet above the ground. They impressed me greatly: the delightfully fragrant odor, the needles and cones on the ground with which Lex [Wilhelmine's brother] and I played, the ceaseless murmur and sighing that I listened to with awe at night as I lay there in the dark before going to sleep.

Part of the farm had been sold to the Credit Valley Railroad for a right-of-way. The deep sandy cut ran along the side of the house not more than 50 feet from it, topped with a good sturdy fence. Lex and I used to climb the fence and watch the train go by every time it passed, and once we were allowed to scramble down the sandy bank to the road bed and walk on the rails to satisfy an urgent curiosity, but had strict orders never to do it without permission.

Grampa worked around home most of the time during this period, but went downtown every day for the paper, *The Galt Reporter*, and the mail. In the evening he sat outdoors under the trees and smoked (it was always summer when I was there). I always enjoyed Grandfather. He looked well — nothing decrepit or aged about him. He would talk to me about the past and present in his slow humorous Scottish voice, with a twinkle in his eye. I can still hear him saying grace at table and reading a chapter from the big family Bible in his rich Scottish brogue before going to bed.

He had not done a very good job, most people thought, and had received few rewards, but he seemed to feel that life had been pretty satisfactory. He did not seem to realize that he had been thoughtless and selfish and had made it very hard for Grandma and his children. They were all good Presbyterians and he went to the "kirk" all his life, listening to sermons hours long about Hell and Damnation, with very little of thoughtfulness and unselfishness. In one of his friendly disposition, and at a time when "everybody was doing it", it is not surprising that he drank too much, but I never heard of him doing a mean or dishonorable thing.

The Ramsays

I do not know when the Ramsays came to Galt — in the early 1830s, no doubt. Grandma's brother, Norman Ramsay, had a contract to build a section of the macadam road in 1837. When I visited them last, at the age of 18, Grandma told me much about the family, and when we went downtown it seemed as though every other person we met was a relation, but I was "too young" to be interested in family and ancestors and did not listen attentively or ask many questions, so I lost my one opportunity of learning facts that I would give a great deal to know now that they are all gone.

Grandma had a sister, Jean, who was the mother of Dr. Neil Macphater who became a noted surgeon and married Sara Halt, daughter of John Halt, known in the United States as the Rubber King until the amalgamation of the rubber trust.

James Ramsay, a nephew, was a fine, good-looking young man, who visited us in Parry Sound one summer and was a great favorite.

When I visited them last, Grandma seemed very old to me, but could not have been more than 66. She was a little stoop-shouldered and wore a lace cap. When we went to town, she wore a bonnet and shawl, and she did not smile very much as we walked along the streets. Grandma would say, "Now, that man is your Father's cousin ... this one is his uncle ... "

James Ramsay, a cousin of Father's, came to see

16

us in Parry Sound. He was rather tall and slim, good-looking and good-natured. I liked him. He was about 21 or 22, and was attending a teacher's college, I think, but I never heard anything more about him.

Galt

The township of Dumfries, in which the town of Galt is situated, was originally part of the lands granted by the British Crown to the Iroquois, or Six Nation, Indians at the close of the American Revolution. This grant on the River Grand was the principle reservation and the chief mustering place of the tribes. It extended on either side of the river for six miles "from its source to its mouth", and the place where Galt now stands was one of their favorite camping grounds.

The forest primeval, the scores of wigwams lining the river banks, the hundreds of painted red men with the other surroundings of semi-savage life, which then frequently filled up the beautiful valley in which Galt is situated, must have made a wonderfully picturesque scene.

Block number 1 — 94,305 acres, now called Dumfries Township — was sold in 1798 by Colonel Brant, for the Indians, to Phillip Steadman, who sold it in 1816 to William Dickson, a native of Dumfrieshire, Scotland, who came to Canada in 1793. The management of the property was given over to a young carpenter from Buffalo, New York, named Absalom Shade. He was tall, wiry, straight as an arrow, with sharp, regular features and sharp, bluish-grey eyes, every inch of him the typical "live Yankee" minus the dyspepsia, slang, and chewing tobacco (so says Mr. Young).

Dickson and Shade were the founders of Galt. Shade lived there the rest of his life, and in the early days the village was known as "Shade's Mills". By 1820, there were only ten buildings: a store, saw mill, flour mill, blacksmith shop, distillery, and the rest crude dwellings.

There was also a bridge across the Grand River, which was for many years the only place where the settlers could cross during high water, and it brought many people from miles up and down the river to the village.

The land around Shade's Mills was thickly timbered, hilly and rugged, in some places stony, with small lakes and swamps scattered throughout. It was not the place for a man afraid of hard work. The soil, however, was excellent for the growth of wheat and other cereals, and when once cleared was unsurpassed for farming purposes in general.

In 1825, settlers began to arrive in greater numbers, almost exclusively Scotlanders from Roxborough and Selkirkshire, where Mr. Dickson advertised his lands extensively, sending articles to *The Chambers Journal* and the regular press about the township and village, and writing freely to leading Scotsmen on the subject. Among others, he corresponded with James Hogg, the Ettrick Shepherd, our worthy and famous ancestor, who was much interested and secured many of the best settlers. A nephew and niece of his own, Samuel Hogg and his sister, Mrs. James Dalgleich, were among the early arrivals. At one time there was some hope that the poet himself might be tempted to cross the water, but when Mr. Dickson offered him a farm in Dumfries, he laughingly replied, "The Yarrow couldna want me," and that was final.

The energy and industry, stimulated by poverty it must be confessed, soon found witness in the disappearing forest: the ax of the woodman, the falling timber, and the merry "yo-heave" of the "raising bee", could be heard on all sides. Many of them owned little but their trusty axes. Their first endeavors were usually to get in a few acres of wheat and to erect a house or shanty, invariably of unhewn logs chinked with clay. There were seldom any divisions except the loft above, but whatever else they lacked, there was always a large fireplace, whose huge blazing back-logs served to distract attention from the earthen floor and threw a ruddy glow of heat and comfort around the primitive apartment and its occupants.

Being all alike poor and more or less dependent on each other, the early pioneers were always open-handed and ready to assist their neighbors. Money was rarely seen, but fortunately the farmers soon had an abundance to eat and not a little to barter in exchange for their other wants.

In 1827, the community was thrown into pleasurable excitement by the arrival of John Galt, founder of Guelph, and party. Mr. Galt was a school companion of Mr. Dickson in Edinboro, who was acting as Commissioner of the Canada Company, the object of his visit being to open up a road from Shade's Mills to the Company's lands near Guelph. His pleasing manners made him quite popular in the village, and when a post office was obtained, Mr. Dickson christened it Galt after his old friend, which settled the much discussed question of a name. Mr. Galt is the father of Sir A. T. Galt of Montreal, and Judge Galt of Toronto. He may have also had more children.

The circumstances of the people began to improve visibly about 1830, the year after my Great-grandfather Francis Hogg with his wife and two sons arrived from Scotland, but many hard struggles were still before them. They were hopeful and cheerful, however, with no lack of good humor and jollity, which is, they say, peculiarly characteristic of Canadian backwoods life. The hard work of chopping, logging, and brush-burning seemed to add zest to social gatherings. Every raising bee terminated in mirth-making of some description. The long winter evenings were often "beguiled" with dancing in which all ages and classes united after the Scottish fashion. Quilting bees also contributed to the comfort and sociability. Toward fall there was hunting. Waterfowl, partridges, foxes, mink, and deer were abundant, and there was good fishing, especially in the smaller streams, which were full of brook trout.

The winter was, as it continues to be, the liveliest season of the year in Canada. The snowfall was abundant, the sleighing steady and good, and the farmers could get their crops to market when the Frost King had paved the roads.

Sad to relate, the baneful custom of drinking was all but universal. The distillery was profitable even when whiskey was only 20 cents a gallon. The quantity consumed, especially on Fair Day when all the countryside was in town, would be considered enormous now. It was regarded as a want of hospitality not to offer visitors a drink, and at marriages and christenings, even at funerals, the black bottle made its appearance. At harvest time, which lasted four or five weeks, workmen regarded their employer a very mean man if a "horn" was not forthcoming every few hours. They lived hard, strenuous lives with food scarce at first, and no variety, little fruit or vegetables, no ice, no luxuries, and "everybody was doing it" — an excuse, but not a reason.

The first settlers of Galt were generally of a superior class, and as early as 1834 they had a debating society. The debates on many subjects, which in the absence of candles took place by the light of burning pine knots, were characterized by deep interest and not a little talent; to use the language of one of the participants, "nothing could exceed the enjoyment of these gatherings." The annual dinner of the Debaters was an occasion never to be forgotten. The dinner was good, but it was the "feast of reason and flow of soul" that filled them with delight. Mr. Young says, "The old pioneers who came into Canada in those early days are our true Canadian heroes."

There was school teaching and irregular religious services from the first, but it was fifteen years before a regularly placed clergyman was obtained. In 1830, the first church was built by the United Presbyterians. (Dr. McMichael's father received a call to this church later, and almost went to Galt.) The attendance upon "religious ordinances", after proper places of worship were obtained, was large and regular. The foundation of old Knox Church, to which our family belonged, was not laid until 1845. It was demolished in 1878, and a fine new church dedicated. It was erected by Dr. Bayne, who first came to Galt in 1835, whose long and eloquent sermons Grandfather, as a boy, listened to every Sabbath, sometimes from 11 A.M. to 3 P.M. Dr. Bayne's picture, an engraving, still hangs on the wall of our old home at Rose Point. He was a man of fine presence, great talent, and noble aims, and the wonder is that he preferred Galt in the backwoods of Canada to the intellectual centers in Europe, in which he was so well fitted to shine. The "new" Knox Church is the only one I can remember, but evidently I was christened in the "auld Kirk" when I was six weeks old in 1873. I wore a daintily embroidered christening robe a yard and a quarter long with ruffled petticoats underneath. Knox Church at that time had a thousand members, the largest congregation in Canada.

The first school house was the result of a bee and was a diminutive log building, but education advanced steadily, and the three "R's" were well taught, no time being frittered away on physiology, botany, or philosophical abstractions, and it is singular, Mr. Young says in 1880, "that the scholar in those little log schools compares favorably in education and advancement with those turned out under our modern system."

A band was organized early, consisting of only three members at first, and a subscription and circulating library, which became an efficient and useful institution. Great-grandfather Francis Hogg and grandfather James Hogg were among those who took an active part in the management of the library.

The Curling Club dates from 1838, and from that day to this, Galt has never been without a flourishing Curling Club. [Curling is a game originating in Scotland and played on ice, in which two teams of four men each slide heavy stones toward a target circle. –Ed.]

The buoyancy of spirits that characterized the community at this period overflowed in another direction and resulted in the formation of a dramatic company, and called for all sorts of talent, including the handling of the paint brush in producing scenery for the various plays and comedies that were presented. It furnished amusement and interest for many years and often assisted deserving institutions in the village with contributions of money.

Galt was incorporated as a village in 1850. Today it is a lovely little city of about 12,000 inhabitants, popularly called the "Gem City of Grand River Valley." The chief industries are flour, cereal, saw, planing, woollen and silk mills, brass and iron foundries, iron and woodworking machinery works, edge tool works, a glove factory, engine, boiler, and sheet metal works, underwear and shoe factories, etc., "and it may be said, without exaggeration, that there are few places anywhere, the masses of whose people are richer, better educated, or more happily situated than they are."

Waterloo

Ten or twelve miles to the northwest of Galt is Waterloo, another spot where civilization began in Canada. The people who pioneered there were largely German. It was as German as Galt was Scotch. To this town came my maternal grandfather, Henry Breimer from Bierfelden, Hesse-Darmstadt, Germany.

The Breimers were cloth manufacturers and of the upper middle class. A Lutheran minister of Waterloo went to Germany on a visit and called on members of our family. He said that nearly everyone in the town was related to the Breimers. There was one "Von", the head of the family, whom he called on and whom he found dressed in hunting costume and surrounded by dogs, horses, and friends, ready for the hunt.

Henry was the second son, and married Wilhelmina Menges, whose family was much farther down the social scale. Henry is said to have quarreled with his older brother and possibly thought he had killed him. He disappeared, leaving his wife, four-year-old son, and little daughter.

The daughter was Marie Sophia Breimer, born in Bierfelden, Germany, in 1851, and my mother. [Note that Wilhelmine sometimes spelled her mother's names Marie and sometimes Mary, sometimes Sophia and sometimes Sophie. –Ed.]

Henry went to Rotterdam and took passage on a boat sailing for Canada. In Waterloo, Ontario, he had a cousin, Carl Mueller, a cooper, who, with his wife,

25

had gone to Canada several years before and now had a good business, a home, and four children, so Henry went straight to them.

He was weeks on the ocean, and on Good Friday ran into a severe storm. Henry feared he would never see his wife and children again. He prayed and promised if he were spared to see them again, he would always, in memory and thankfulness, fast on that day, and as long as he lived, he never failed to fast on Good Friday from sundown to sundown.

The following year, Wilhelmina (Grandma), Frederick (Uncle Fred), and Marie (my Mother) sailed from Rotterdam to join him in Canada. They were three weeks on the ocean. Mother could remember how rough it was and how the ship rolled and tossed. It was probably 1854 or '55.

He had bought five acres of land on the outskirts of town, which he farmed most efficiently the rest of his life. He built a frame house, which was comfortable, but not well arranged according to the ideas of the 1900s. It never had a coat of paint, but was weathered a soft grey, and looked like the houses I saw in the Amana German settlement in Iowa.

He laid out his land: an apple orchard, a small hay field, a large patch of strawberries, a vegetable garden, a barn, and yard with grape arbors, fruit trees, small fruits, flowers in every available corner, and a huge brick bake oven. There were also chickens, geese, and a cow. It was hard work, and he had to work also in a woollen mill at times to make a little extra money, but he never ceased to resent being a common laborer with other men over him. Farming was different. It was dignified and independent.

Grandfather was of medium height, thin and dark. I think Mother looked more like him than like Grandmother. They said he was part French from Alsace-Lorraine.

But the small farm, though it flourished, was never enough to supply his growing family. Five more children were born — Carrie, Bertha, and Sarah, and two boys, William and Henry. They all worked very hard on their small farm, and it surprises me now how much they raised on it.

The boys, Fred, William, and Henry Jr., left home as soon as possible, going to the larger cities: Hamilton, Ontario, Buffalo, and Detroit. The daughters, Carrie, Bertha, and Sarah stayed at home in the little old weathered house, but Marie, the eldest (my Mother), was for a time in Buffalo, and later went to Galt to keep house for her brother, Fred, during a short residence there. Fred, at 16, was a drummer boy in the American Army during the Civil War. He married Aunt Katie and went to live in Hamilton, where his two daughters, Elfreda (Elfie) and Gertie, were born. When they were still very young, he died, and Aunt Katie moved to Detroit, and there they lived for many years. Elfie still lives there. Gertie lives now in California.

The original house in Waterloo was never enlarged or painted, to my knowledge, but it always seemed a pleasant place to me, especially outdoors. Grandma and the aunties were kind and indulgent to us children, and there were geese and chickens, cows and pigs, which created much activity and interest for us.

How they could do so much on such a small place is a wonder. The long arbor hung with luscious grapes. We played under it, and could eat all we wanted. Along its side were four tall pear trees, on the other side of the small lawn were plum trees, and near the house were cherry trees — all bearing loads of delicious fruit. There were early dewy mornings when the acre of strawberries was picked and carried to market, yellow apples in the orchard, radishes and new onions in the vegetable garden, with currant and raspberry bushes around the edge of it. On baking day, when the brick oven was heated, huge loaves of bread, beautifully browned on top, came out of it, and coffee cakes, schnitz pies, and cookies — enough to last a large family for days.

The first Christmas that I remember was spent there. Early in the morning before dawn, we were carried into the "parlor" — Lex and I — and there was a large tree gaily decorated with small Christmas cakes with colored icing, nuts and seeds sprinkled over them, silvered [slivered] nuts, red apples, sticks of red and white candy, and small gifts. Larger gifts were laid around underneath — my china doll dressed completely in white with blue ribbons. I do not remember what we did or said, and wonder if we fulfilled the grownup's anticipations, but it made a deep impression on me and is one of my clearest memories.

On Easter morning following, we were up at dawn and out to see what the rabbits had left us. Sure enough, there under the peony bushes were two large nests overflowing with beautifully colored eggs, and we were sure we had seen the rabbit skipping around the corner just as we came out of the door.

Uptown in Waterloo, the German language and broken English were heard everywhere, and it had the appearance of a German town. When I think of it, I smell cabbage, sauerkraut, bologna, and beer. There were large breweries, and the brewers' big horses, with wagons piled high with kegs, were seen everywhere, and beer was sold in so many places that as you walked along the street the prevailing odor was of beer. I never saw any at Grandma's, but no doubt they drank it at times.

The children got only the schooling that the public school and the Lutheran Church offered.

Mother, as the oldest girl, was soon doing all the family sewing, and for so many that was a lot. "Inchie" Van Chultus came to live with them and was like one of the family. She was really a boarder in Grandmother's care, and since she was only a child, we were together a lot when I was there, and I thought she was fine. She lived with them for years — now lives in Toronto, married, and has a son. Aunt Sarah sees her often.

Aunt Carrie married a Scotsman also, William McLachlan, a foundry man. Their children were: Wilhelmina, called Willo, who married Bruce Robinson; Mamie, who married Cort(?) Pavey, and lives in Los Angeles with a daughter; Beth and Berta Sinclair, and Clyde. They all live in the West now, in Vancouver and vicinity and Los Angeles. Aunt Carrie died in 193?, many years after her husband.

Aunt Bert married an Irishman, Will Sterling. Their children are Will, Katherine ("Girlie"), Sam, Vera, and Wilhelmina. Aunt Bert and the girls live in Los Angeles also.

Sarah married a German, Albert Dunke; their children: Floyd, Loraine, who is now Mrs. Wallace Robinson, and Carl, all of Toronto. A. K. Dunke died several years ago.

Every one of the sons and sons-in-law of the Breimer family have died, while five of the daughters and daughters-in-law still live.

Grandma Breimer was a dear grandma, so kind and good to us. On Sundays I went to the Lutheran Church with her. She was all dressed in black "with a touch of yellow."

Grandma Breimer's maiden name was Wilhelmina Menges. Her mother, Magdalina Menges, came to Canada with her, and I went to her funeral but do not remember her at all, and know nothing about the family.

[Remember that this is being written in 1938. –Ed.]

My Mother and Father

Francis Ramsay Hogg, son of James and Barbara Ramsay Hogg, was born in Galt, Ontario, on July 7, 1845. [Note: Wilhelmine spelled her father's middle name two ways, as with her mother's name. It was sometimes Ramsey and sometimes Ramsay. I even have two calling cards, one with Ramsey and one with Ramsay. My father insists the name was spelled Ramsay. He said the Ramsey name was lower class. –Ed.]

His schooling was limited to the crude little school houses that his father and grandfather had helped to "raise" in the pioneer days of Galt. The teachers were anyone they could get, but there seems to have been many natural-born teachers among them, for he got a good solid foundation of reading, 'riting, and 'rithmetic. With his inherited love of learning and books they had and the debating society, many of the scholars of those first little school houses "compare favorably in education and advancement with those turned out under our modern system," Mr. Young says. If the urgent need of earning a living and being his mother's right hand had not come to him so early in life, he would have been a good student and gone as far as any of them.

As it was, Father was a good reader. He had a nice voice and read easily and naturally, with good pronunciation and inflection, an accomplishment which many of the college graduates of today have failed to acquire. He read the Bible aloud regularly and what interested him in the newspapers each evening, and once he read a whole book aloud. The book he read was *The Scottish Chiefs*. I can understand why he never did it again, remembering the confusion of one reading lamp, so many children studying and doing homework, asking questions, and just talking. Also after he had looked over the paper, *The Globe*, he was too tired to do anything but go to bed.

Dad's handwriting, too, was especially nice, I always thought. It had a style all its own. His bookkeeping was neat and correct. He was always interested in world affairs, kept right up with the times, and could express himself well.

I remember him best as a young man, as I saw very little of him after I left home at the age of 20 and went so far away that I returned home only for short vacations. I regret that now, and sometimes think that a young person should think twice before giving up family, friends, and country to make a home with strangers. Loyalty and love are divided, and sometimes when a choice has to be made, it is very hard.

Father was of medium height, with dark hair and grey eyes. He dressed as well as most men in the town, and compared favorably in general appearance. I thought he was nice looking, myself.

And he had all the faults and virtues of his ancestors. His faults – now that I try to name them I find it difficult, for he hadn't any bad ones. We thought he was pretty hard on us sometimes, and somehow we got the idea that he was to blame when things were unpleasant. The influence of the "auld kirk" was strong. He was brought up on such rules as "spare the rod and spoil the child," "no whusseling on Sunday," "no playing for keeps." Never having had much childhood himself, he did not always understand or appreciate his small playful boys.

But he was true to his family and really devoted at heart. He had dreams of being able to give us all the things he thought we should have.

He played a good game of checkers, but would have nothing to do with cards or liquor. So he never learned any smart tricks or "finesse."

In the early days of Parry Sound, he enjoyed curling during the winter when he was in the office most of the time. His natural good nature and social tendencies were dampened by the constant grind and lack of success in a financial way, for he would have been a most interesting companion if he had had a little more leeway.

He was culler and shipper for the Parry Sound Lumber Company. He was at the mill at 6am and worked until 6pm, with an hour at noon, which left little time for anything else. He liked his job as a lumberman — the big trees felled in the bush, floated down the river, sawed into lumber, piled in the lumber yards, and loaded on the boats that sailed away to Tonawanda and other American ports. I can see him now, with a sturdy yard measure with a brass attachment to turn over the boards in his hand, inspecting each board, and supervising the men who were loading the boat.

Like all his ancestors, he loved the country — the hills, woods, and streams. On Sunday afternoon, he would take us children for a walk to the top of one of our hills and sit there for a while looking across the Sound and around its rockbound, tree-bordered shore, or over the harbor surrounded with mills and lumber yards, and across to Rosette and Sloop Islands, and beyond Parry Sound, the Indian Reservation — and dream.

I would like to know now all he dreamed. He was always a good hard worker, honest and interested, but always a dreamer, I suspect, as I am, with no idea how to make money other than his daily wage, which was never enough. I am hoping that now he understands and sees this — not as a frustration of hopes — but as an accomplishment in spite of everything, and necessary to the final attainment.

On Sunday we all went to the little Presbyterian Church. It was small and plain as a church could be, yet it had a dignity and impressiveness that I have seldom felt since. Dad led us to our seat — second from the front — and let us all pass in, he and Mother sitting at the end next to the aisle. Sometimes he helped take up the collection. Until some of us went up to sing in the choir, there were ten of us.

My mother, Mary, was a very pretty, bright, clever girl, more like her father, and naturally refined though uneducated and untrained except for the ways of a German household, including sewing and dressmaking, a very few years of attendance at the common school, and the Lutheran Church. When she went to Galt, it was not long before the gay Marie and the young Scotch Presbyterian Frank Hogg were attracted to each other. Mary longed for something more substantial and serious in her life, and Frank needed more beauty and gaity in his.

Soon they were married, July 11, 1870.

Mother made her own wedding dress, which was of mauve silk, with bell sleeves, and trimmed with a little real lace. She was so busy dressing up her whole family for the occasion and looking after the hundred and one things that had to be attended to that she was almost late for her own wedding. I think of it now when I see girls feted and relieved of all responsibility and work, their only thought to look their best and enjoy all the excitement.

Marie looked so pretty, however, that the local photographer insisted on taking her picture, for which we are deeply grateful to him now. My daughter, Marion, had it enlarged and done in colors by an artist in New York and put it in a small gold frame. It is perfect and one of my most prized possessions. Marion gave it to me on Mother's Day.

They were married in Waterloo, and soon after went to the little cottage on South Water Street, Galt, where I was born.

The mill was farther down on South Water Street, which ran along the banks of the Grand River. I know very little about those first years. Much as they cared for each other, there was friction. One cause was Marie's sisters coming to visit them, and always talking in German. If you have ever heard German women talking and gossiping together, not understanding the language, you know it can sound pretty awful. They talked and talked even when Dad was around, and that always annoyed him, knowing as he did that in their hearts they were critical of the strange ways of the Scotch and the Hoggs in particular. Then, money was scarce and there were many bills to pay for two families. There was also a difference of opinion as to what was necessary to buy and what was not, and Mother would lie in bed listening to Dad and his mother talking, while she imagined all sorts of things.

But they loved each other to the very end, in spite of the conflicts between their natures and upbringing. They did not compromise and "blend" enough. Though admiring the other, each wanted the other to be different, to live and think differently. So there was conflict and a division in our really devoted family, though

Mother became a strong Presbyterian, worked hard and long with little complaint, and won the love and admiration of her children and her friends.

She and Father had a few years alone together at Ettrick. Father was sick, and Mother, alone in that rather lonely spot, had to care for Dad and do almost everything else herself. We children were scattered over the face of the continent and not seeming to be able to go to them. It was hard, but one good thing came out of it: they learned again to appreciate each other, to know that they loved, and always had loved, each other.

When Dad passed away in January, 1917, I think he must have felt satisfied and ready to go. Mary, though exhausted after the months of day and night "duty", felt satisfied that she had done what she could, and that whatever the misunderstandings, and self-ishness caused by ignorance, of the past, they had been able to see through the difficulties — the why and wherefore of them — and to forgive.

Mary lived twenty years after Frank's death, a charming, gracious, intelligent "old lady", who was much loved and admired by all who knew her. Pleas-ant to live with, helpful, and entertaining, her children welcomed her to their homes, and even the young grandchildren, who are so often impatient, though tolerant, were proud to introduce her to their friends and enjoyed having her around. "Gram" we called her, and treated her like a chum. She was interested in everything, and busy every minute, helping here and there, working among her flowers, sewing, crocheting, reading, and writing letters.

When her time came in her 84th year, she was in excellent health, working for hours outdoors, taking long walks, spending days in town, and doing everything the rest of us were doing. Her intellect and hearing were unimpaired, and she needed glasses only for close work. That last morning she was up as usual, and went out in the garden for a few minutes and then returned to her bedroom. When she did not come to breakfast, we went to call her and found her lying on the bed apparently asleep.

We took her back to the old home; the services were held in the old church she had loved so well; many old friends were there with her, a few relatives, and three of her own children. It was a beautiful, friendly service; she would have loved it. On a wooded hillside, as the sun was sinking low on an April evening, she was laid beside Father, and the roses were strewn over them both. It was ideal.

I will never be afraid of it again.

My Brothers and Sisters

I am the oldest — Wilhelmine Ramsay, born September 5, 1873, Galt, Ontario.

Second, Alexander Blake, born November 27, 1876, in Cargill, Ontario.

Third, Christina Colene, born August 4, 1878, in Parry Sound, Ontario.

Fourth, Charlotte Bertha, born March 15, 1881, in Parry Sound, Ontario.

Fifth, James Henry, born June 25, 1883, in Parry Harbor, Ontario.

Sixth, Frank Breimer, born December 10, 1885, in Parry Harbor, Ontario.

Seventh, Frederick Archibald, born February 9, 1888, in Parry Harbor, Ontario.

Eighth, Oliver Mowatt, born February 14, 1891 in Parry Harbor, Ontario.

Lex

Brother Lex, Alexander Blake, was born in that little lumber town in Bruce County, Ontario, called then Yoccasippi, now Cargill, on November 27, 1875. He walked when he was ten months old, and before we left there when he was two years old, he ran down that stony hill "helter skelter" to the crude little church at the foot of it. I can see him going, and we held our breath for fear he would fall, but can't remember that he ever did.

He went through the public school in Parry Sound and began early to work in the lumber yard in the summer time. His first real job was in the Bank of Ottawa, where he worked for several years, taking on the appearance and manners of a bank clerk. He looked so nice in his navy blue double-breasted suits that he wore generally, and he had a good time entering into all the social activities of the old town.

Later he was sent to the Bank in the City of Ottawa and joined a Regiment of some kind there. But the progress financially was too slow for him and he began to dream of "going West" where fortunes were made in short order. So he left the Bank and took a trip around calling on relatives and friends, and extended it to Chicago where I was living at the time. He thought he might get into something there with the aid of some friends, but finally gave it up and went west to British Columbia, settling in time at Kamloops where he started an insurance and land (?) business and married his pretty office assistant.

They have three boys: Bruce is in a bank in Vancouver; Billy was for a time on a big boat between British Columbia and China, but now is going into the army to fight for the British Empire and Freedom (he became a navigator in the Royal Canadian Air Force in West Coast Defense); Charlie is already in England with his regiment, "The Seaforth Highlanders". He is a handsome lad in his uniform, according to the photo he sent his Aunt Colene. So we are in the war again personally, hoping and praying that Charlie will come through it and return safely to his father and mother. I have never seen any of them, not even my brother since he visited me in Chicago.

Lex died in Kamloops, British Columbia, in October, 1941. Charlie was in England at the time. Billy was able to go home, but arrived too late.

Colene

Christina Colene was born in Parry Sound, August 4, 1878, a few months after our arrival there. She had a clear bird-like voice and with few advantages became one of our soloists, singing in the choir and in musical entertainments. She never liked to sew or do "fancy-work" and always traded off even her own mending. She liked active duty and preferred housework and cooking.

Her first trip away from home alone was to Waterloo and Elmira where she stayed with Aunt Sarah for several months. Somehow she finally found an opening in the Sanitorium at Danville, New York, where she took a course in nursing, later going to Waterloo, Iowa, where I was living. There she met Dr. Childs of Cleveland, while nursing his uncle, and they were married August 11, 1902. It was Dr. Childs' second marriage, and he had two little daughters about 6 and 8 who were living with their grandmother in Montpelier, Vermont. Colene and Lyman went to Parry Sound on their wedding trip, to Montreal and Quebec, stopping on their way to Cleveland at Montpelier to pick up their two little girls.

Eleanor was born a year from the following Christmas (December 30, 1903). A son, Lyman Jr., followed, and six years later, on Christmas Day, 1917, the twins were born. Colene was a very busy girl all these years; she had her ups and downs, but money was plenty and regular, though she used comparatively little of it on herself. They went to Rose Point every summer for a vacation of a month or two. This is 1940, and they are there again this summer, having missed only two or three summers in all these years.

In 1935, Lyman gave up his practice and many activities in Cleveland and moved to Florida, where he had several acres planted to citrus fruits, then in full bearing, and a nice comfortable house all ready to move into.

Eleanor is married and has two children, Virginia and Billy, living in Cleveland. Lyman Jr. and his young wife, Marion, live there also. The twins, Martha and Elizabeth, and Frances live together at 3248 Cleveland Heights Blvd., and Evelyn, the eldest of the family has just gone to Albany, New York, where she is accepting a fine position in the hospital there.

Colene is famous for remembering birthdays and other anniversaries. She not only remembers them, but also sends some kind of greeting almost without exception. She also writes many fine letters, and has done more to keep the family together than anyone else in it.

She knows all the roads up and down and cross-ways through the country by name and number, and has such a reliable sense of direction and location that she is accepted as an authority on all the automobile trips she goes on no matter who is at the wheel. Maps are her delight, and she collects them and refers to and studies them constantly. She enjoys travel and new places so intensely and tells about what she sees so well, never seeming to be really satisfied, that her friends often say, "If I ever can do it I am going to give you money for a trip around the world." Lately she has gone long distances by bus, and Evelyn said, "That is just what she should be – a bus driver. Or a guide on personally conducted tours," and later Colene herself wondered if she could not get a station wagon and pay for it by taking passengers to town on regular trips.

Lyman loves it in Florida, but Colene is restless unless some of her family are here very often. They come for Christmas in bunches of three or four, and sometimes again at Easter vacation, and she goes north in June and often does not return until late in the fall, going to Parry Sound for a month in the summer and on other side trips. Her children and grandchildren all being in Cleveland, her interests and her heart are mostly there also. I miss her when she is gone, as she comes over often and always brings interesting letters or news or takes me with her in the car to market or wherever she is going.

Charlotte

Charlotte Bertha came to us on March 15, 1881. Her head was covered with dark curls, which — even now that they are white — are a crowning beauty. She went to school, church, and singing school with the rest of us, took part in and enjoyed all the activities of our little community.

She was at home with Mother long after Colene and I had departed, Lex and Jim also, and helped her take care of the house, the three youngest boys, and Father. During the summers the Childs family would be there with them for two or three months, and when "Lottie" did leave the old home about 1903, she went to Cleveland to live with them and assist Colene with her large family. Later she came to Sioux City where we were living, and there she met J.H. Corbin, whom she married.

They went west to Montana for a while. Young Jack was born, and they returned to Sioux City where they lived until they came to Florida in 1926. Jack, Jr. was (?) years old, Bettie, 5, and Jean, 2. That was fourteen years ago.

Jack now is a tall good-looking young man. He graduated from high school at a time when this country — indeed the whole world — was going through a Depression from which we have not yet recovered. The most tragic thing about it has been the thousands of young men graduating from schools, colleges, and universities, brimful of life and ambition, but with no jobs or opportunities in sight. They were disheartened, frustrated, not able to marry; the only way for many to exist was to "go on relief".

Jack finally solved his problem by shipping on a tanker sailing between Boston and New York and Texas, Aruba, and other oil points around the Caribbean. He is still with the Standard Oil Company, but at present is going to a maritime school where he has to study hard — on what, his Mother does not know, as Jack is not long on explanations. He took a course in radio before he sailed. Since oil is not being shipped to European ports and because of other disorganization, sixty or more tankers are tied up in New York Harbor, which may account for the three months' schooling.

Jack took one trip to Hamburg, Germany. He earns a good salary, spends little on the boat, much more probably during his long ... [Unfortunately, the rest of the pages about Charlotte and her family are missing. –Ed.]

Frank

Frank Breimer Hogg was born in Parry Sound, Ontario, Canada, December 10, 1886, the sixth baby in our family. He was a very attractive baby, and I was always proud to take him out in the baby buggy. He finished in the public school and went early to work in the lumber yards, camps, and railroads until in 1904 he went to Cleveland, Ohio, worked in a machine shop, and lived with the Childs (our sister, Colene).

About 1907 he came to Sioux City, Iowa, where we [Wilhelmine, her husband, and their children, Dick, my father Ralph, and Marion. –Ed.] were living, and later went with us to South Dakota where we took up a claim five miles east of Hermosa. He had a horse and loved to ride over those prairies in the shadow of Mt. Harney. He had a job at one of the ranches and enjoyed the life very much, I think. When we returned to Sioux City, he went West to Washington State and settled in or near Underwood and White Salmon where he had friends. He helped run a grocery store for a while, worked in apple orchards, and carried mail for a while. Then he went to live and work with Mr. Brooks. They were from Boston and had a very nice home. One daughter, Rae, lived there with them.

The first World War started, and our youngest brother enlisted at once in the Canadian Army. He went through it without a scratch until March 24, 1917, when he was killed on sharp-shooting duty at St. Elois. Soon after, the United States declared war on

Germany, and Frank felt he wanted to go and avenge his brother's death. We were all feeling so badly that it seemed natural that he felt like that. So he joined up and was sent to Camp Lewis. Before he left camp he and Rae were married. In the Rose Parlor, Benson Hotel, Portland, Oregon, December 24 at noon, they were married, and Frank was the happiest man in Camp Lewis. Thirty of the boys took out licenses that day.

He changed the spelling of his name that day to Hogue, so he was Sgt. F. B. Hogue, "L" Co., 361st Infantry, A.E.F.

Fritz, Ollie, And Lottie

Frederick Archibald Hogg, who was always called Fritz as a boy, was a small thin child, but healthy and very active, always getting into mischief. We sent him to the post office one day, and when he was gone longer than necessary, I ran to the corner to see what was keeping him. In front of Ross's store he was talking to a man, who grabbed him by the seat of the pants and held him out at arms length. He was liked by everyone, but was inattentive and playful at school and Sunday School, and couldn't learn his Catechism, which Father undertook to teach him. Dad was impatient, and Fritz's Sunday afternoons were ruined by that Catechism. He worked at Depot Harbor, also, but soon went to Cleveland to visit the Childs.

He then came over to Sioux City where he lived for a good many years. At first he had one job after another, losing them almost as fast as he got them on account of some kid trick or burst of temper. At last he found a place with the Johnson Biscuit Company and was with them a long time, having learned a few things. He got to be head of a department and a salesman around the city. It was a candy factory, also, and Fred loved chocolates. He could eat as many as he wanted to, and did.

We left Sioux City about that time, and I do not know the details of the next few years, until 1917. Our youngest brother, Ollie, was killed in France that year, and the United States was entering the war. Fred felt

48

that he owed the Germans one on account of Ollie, so he enlisted, and soon was sent to a camp near San Francisco, near the Golden Gate. After a few weeks' training he was sent to France. On account of his eyes, he was not sent to the front, but to the office of a major, where his bookkeeping and nice handwriting were needed. He had one delightful leave down near Spain, I think, and a week in Paris where my husband, David, was at the time. Back in the U.S., he was "demobilized" at Sioux City and walked out a free man again after a year of obeying orders and "never thinking for myself at all", and he says he felt lost for a minute, not knowing what to do next. But he soon adjusted himself and found another job. Then he married Bernice Lewis. They had a nice little home in Morningside and seem to have been very happy.

But Fred began to have trouble with his stomach and had a very bad spell when they thought he could not recover. Ulcers of the stomach, the doctors said. He got over it, but had to diet and be very careful. Bernice was going to have a baby. Both were delighted, and everything seemed perfect, but neither mother nor baby lived through it, and Fred was left heartbroken.

Charlotte and J. H. Corbin lived there then. He took a room with them and went out on the road as salesman for some company. On one of his trips far from home he had another spell. Mother went to be near him, and when he was able to travel, they took him to Cleveland. But he was slow in getting over it, and we invited him to come to Florida. He stayed with us for nearly three years, gaining his health back completely. He helped build our big house, but the Florida slump set in, there was a hurricane, and a few other things that ruined business in Florida, and Fred could not earn a decent living. Mother was here and was going back to Cleveland and Parry Sound for the summer, so Fred took her up in his car and stayed in Cleveland. He had several jobs there before he found the one he liked with a produce company. He got along well there, liked the men he worked for, and was very successful as a salesman around the city. He liked Cleveland, but longed to return to Florida where he had bought three lots on Lake Lucy on which he hoped to build a home some day. Then he found Sue and married her. His stomach still bothered him, and he was reckless when he felt well, so the inevitable occurred. Suddenly he had an attack and was rushed to the hospital, where he died in a short time, April 13, 1938.

Fred was a good tennis player, and after he came to Florida we made a tennis court on which he worked hard and on which he had many a good game. He liked pinochle also and a good cigar or pipe. He was always more or less of a kid, using many slang phrases, but clean as could be in thought, word, and action.

My Memories of Galt

There was the Chicago fire, and the smoke reached Galt. Black specks covered the clothes on the line. That was the year of the last Fenian raid of Canada. Some Irishmen worked at the mill. They were very sullen and talked in low tones, and Mother was afraid of them.

Then there was Father Shenique (spelling?), a Catholic priest in Montreal, who protested against many of the practices of the priests and nuns and wrote a book about it. The Irish Catholics who worked in the mill were wild about it, and when Father Shenique came to Galt to speak, they were ready to kill anyone who went to hear him. Father Shenique then left Canada with all his followers and settled in Kankakee, Illinois, where they joined a Protestant denomination.

1873 was the year of one of the worst depressions and panics. In the midst of it, on September 5, I arrived on the scene. It was so bad that Dad lost his mill and everything else but his two girls. He had had very little business training, and with two families to support, it was soon evident that he would have to give it up. He went with another lumber company to a small lumber town in Bruce County. After a short visit in Waterloo, Mother and I went to him, moving away from Galt before I was two years old.

His new job was with the Diamond Company, in a very small community attached to the mill called then "Yoccasippi" (that is how it sounded), now called

Cargill.

Our house was in a terrace (a string of small houses attached to each other). We were about in the middle. It was small and unattractive.

There my brother, Lex — Alexander Blake — was born November 27, 1876. Being carried upstairs by my Uncle Will to see Mother and my baby brother for the first time is my first definite memory. It was a dreary place with few recollections: Mother kneading bread at the table while I sat at the foot of the cradle with my feet between the spindles rocking the baby to sleep; a boarding house not far away where there were some young people, and where I have a distinct memory of feeling that I was quite popular; Lex, who learned to walk at nine months, running down the stony hill "helter-skelter", as Mother said, to Sunday School.

Dad had been instrumental in getting a small building erected for a Sunday School room, and he was the superintendent. It was a very crude building, built of unplaned lumber and unpainted — yellow and severe. We ran down that hill on a cold and frosty Sunday, climbed the rather steep step at the door and into a room with a red hot stove in the middle. The sap oozed out and ran down the walls and the room smelled strongly of it. There were a few benches and a table, and a lot of children with a few grownups.

Then on a grey cold morning in the fall, we were saying goodbye to our friends and neighbors and soon were in a farm wagon, being driven to the nearest railroad station. We all went to Galt for a few days to see Grandma and Grandpa Hogg, Aunt Maggie, and her family. Dad went from there, I think, to Parry Sound, while we went to Waterloo to spend the winter with Grampa and Gramma Breimer. She was a dear Gramma, so kind and good to us. On Sundays I went to the Lutheran Church with her, she all dressed in black "with a touch of yellow."

As soon as navigation opened up on Georgian Bay, we went to Collingwood and, aboard the "Waubuno", went on to Parry Sound.

Georgian Bay

In July, 1615, Champlain, having traveled all the way from Montreal by way of the Ottawa River, saw before him, to the south and west, a body of water, beautifully blue, extending to the horizon. It was the first of the Great Lakes to be discovered. Today we call it Georgian Bay. His canoes threaded their way through the maze of islands that fringe the northeastern shore of the bay, passed what is now Parry Sound, and went on to Huronia, the land of the Hurons, near Midland to the southeast. Commander Bayfield of the Royal Navy, who was appointed by the Canadian government to make a survey of Lake Huron and Georgian Bay in 1822, discovered that beautiful sheet of landlocked water when he rounded the point now known as Killbear Point, and named it Parry Sound after Sir William Edward Parry, the Arctic explorer.

Georgian Bay has area and depth, qualifying it to rank as one of the Great Lakes, and the people living on its shores never think of it as being part of Lake Huron. There is good reason for this. It is 120 miles long and about 50 wide from the eastern shore to Grand Manitoulin Island, but the whole region as far up the shore as the "Soo" is of the same formation and seems to belong all together. Manitoulin is 107 miles long and from 4 to 25 miles wide, the whole of these shores as full of fjords and inlets as the coast of Norway. Many islands — 30,000 charted -- are strewn along the whole north shore, and the route through them requires great skill and watchfulness to avoid the many rocks and shoals, but they are also a shelter in time of storm.

Through this whole region, which is in the great Laurentian shield lying in a half circle around Hudson Bay, there were originally lofty mountain ranges, so geologists say, thrown up by great internal forces, indicating tremendous convulsions of nature. Ages beyond computation have worn them down to rounded hills and tablelands, covered now to a great extent by forests and much luxuriant vegetation, but the rock is very near the surface and sticks out everywhere. Needless to say it is not a good farming country, and yet the fruits and vegetables and grains grown there are of the best. During the short growing season, seeds planted come up in no time and mature rapidly. Wild berries — raspberries, huckleberries, strawberries, gooseberries, cranberries — are abundant, and rhubarb grows the largest stalks I have ever seen.

From Manitoulin Island to Cabots Head on the Ontario side is a great barrier of rocks, shoals, and islands, almost separating the Bay from Lake Huron. The transition from Georgian Bay to Lake Huron is so sudden as to be startling. Passing through the channel, the scene has completely changed. Before you are broad open waters, with not a sight of the sandy beaches of this lower region, not a rock nor an island – nothing but water. It is no wonder that those who live and labor around the Bay think of it as apart from Lake Huron. It is their own Great all-Canadian Lake.

Sailing across Parry Sound, the ship passes through a narrow channel and enters an inner harbor to the east of it, into which a river flows from the north. There in the valley of the river, surrounded by hills, on a spot that had been an Indian trading post and meeting place, a mill was built. It was the lure and the wealth of the pine trees that brought the lumbermen and civilization to that distant outpost. The river offered water power for saw mills and a waterway down which to float the logs from up the valley. The first sawmill was built in 1857 by J. W. Gibson. It was a small waterpower mill. A dam was built across the river where rapids formed at its mouth, which supplied the power. They built also a blacksmith shop, barn, stable, boarding house, store, and seven or eight log houses.

In 1863, the Gibsons sold their mill to John and William Beatty. The Beattys owned all the land on which the village was built, and large timber limits. William Beatty was always considered the founder and was known as Governor Beatty. He was a man of education, integrity, enterprise, and foresight, and his wife was one of the most perfect ladies I have ever known, in the true sense of the word. She was educated, refined, friendly, and unselfish. She came there as a bride, the daughter of one of Toronto's mayors, Mayor Bowes. She had lived for some time in Paris and spoke French fluently. They belonged to the Methodist Church, and Mrs. Beatty played the organ for years, taught a class in Sunday School, and entered into all activities.

The town site was surveyed, and streets were laid out in regular order, bordered with maple trees. It was named Parry Sound. The Beattys were naturally against the liquor traffic, and Gov. Beatty had a clause inserted in all deeds stipulating that no liquor should be sold on the land "on pain of forfeiture." This clause has never been successfully contested, and the main part of town is today without a place where liquor can be bought. Of course, licenses have been granted in the next township on the outskirts of Parry Sound, but as the place is strung out along the harbor with hills between, it is a long way to go for a drink, and the children grow up with no saloons in sight nor drunken men around. Law is law, in Canada.

The maple trees were quite large and shady when we arrived. The roads, of course, were unpaved — pure unadulterated sand, but there were board crossings and sidewalks on the main streets. There were two general stores, belonging to the lumber companies, well stocked with everything needful; also meat markets, shoe stores, drug store, watch repair, millinery, one bookstore (Mr. Holmes' bookstore where we got all our slates, pencils, and books; also our Christmas cards and Valentines), and other things.

The only hotel was the Seguin House on the corner of Seguin Street and James Street. It was a homey looking place, more like a boarding house, and was run by the Kirkman family, whose daughter, Ellen, was my first teacher in school, whom I admired so much.

There were three churches: Methodist, Presbyterian, and Episcopal or, as we called it, The Church of England. There was a public hall, called Jukes' Music Hall after the man who owned it.

The three lumber mills with their lumber yards and the public docks occupied the shore line on three sides of the Harbor, the south side being still beautifully natural. A grist mill was built over rapids a mile up the Seguin River. At the mouth of the river was the big watermill where Dad worked. There was a dam across the river mouth with spillways and chutes to carry the logs. The river was divided by a wooden floating walk. There was a bridge farther up the river connecting Seguin Street with the road on the east side. I crossed that bridge thousands of times going to church, school, and almost every other place I went. We first lived for several years on the west side, but when Dad lost his job because he didn't vote for Mr. Miller, the president of the Parry Sound Lumber Company, we went over to the Midland and North Shore on the east side of the Harbor, and we lived over there near the office and mill and crossed the bridge daily.

Parry Sound

Parry Sound was an interesting place, and the people we found there were remarkable. Separated from the "outside" civilized world by sixty miles of water, with 75 miles of very rough country from the nearest railroad, with six or seven months of winter when the Bay was frozen over, and the only way either out or in was over that long rough road by stage, it was no place for the soft or timid. The men and women who went there to make their homes were pioneers and adventurers at heart. They had individuality, ideas, and purpose, and were naturally intelligent. A few were well educated and had world-wide interests.

They were mill owners and managers, men of strong personality and ability; teachers in the school, one after another teaching me a little bit of truth and giving me another outlook on the great wide world, each one meaning something very special to me even now; ministers and their families, seeming more than usual to work together irrespective of denomination; doctors and lawyers, who came in those early days and stayed on the rest of their days, among our best and most cherished friends; merchants stayed, too, but the bankers and the bank clerks and office men came and went. The new personalities were always refreshing and gave a more leisurely social air to our lives.

Miss Hicock, who taught piano and voice, was for years our leader in all musical undertakings. To her we owe the little we know about music, and especially our appreciation of good music. I personally owe her much more than that, for I spent much time in her sister's home where she lived. It was one of the nicest homes in town, and they were fine cultured people with a good sense of humor. I learned there to appreciate more all the nice ways of saying and doing things. We had so much fun in their house. It was quite large, and besides the musicals and other entertainments and parties, we could romp all over the place, playing hide-and-seek, pussy-wants-a-corner, and charades, grown-ups and all. We learned our parts there and were drilled in the choruses of the little operas we "put on": "The Coronation of the Rose", "HMS Pinafore", "Cinderella", "Prince Puss-in-Boots", "The Mikado", and others.

Of all that "merrie companie", only one still lives there in Parry Sound: Mrs. Walter Foote, who was one of our best alto soloists, still lives in her pleasant home on Belvedere Hill.

The Hill spread over a large area. It had been covered with trees, but they had been cut down, leaving many stumps. The rock formations appeared everywhere, smooth and rounded, with grass and shrubs between and many junipers. Up that hill we climbed many Sunday afternoons with Dad. At the top nearest the town was a tower called the "Observatory", for observation of weather conditions and the flying of signals and warnings. It was planted on a solid rock of granite with wide seams of white crystal tinged with white and black, and sheets of mica that we could peel off. There were large boulders scattered around and many beautiful stones that we played with by the hour, and we always carried as many as we could home for Mother's "rockery". We could see the harbor from there, but the Sound was obscured by the trees that grew around the edge on the slope to the water. It was quite a walk to the high bluff overlooking the Sound and the sunset. A hotel was later built just where we used to sit, called "The Belvedere" and that section became one of the nicest residential parts of the town.

My Childhood in Parry Sound

The Waubuno was a chunky little side-wheeler that made regular weekly trips from Southport to points on the North Shore, carrying mail, passengers, and freight. On a day early in May, 1878, she hauled in her gang-plank and lines and slowly moved away from the dock on one of her first trips of the season. It was cold, though sunny, and there were few passengers, as travel for pleasure had not yet begun that season. But Mother, Lex, and I were going home.

We had never seen it, but Father was there. He was employed by one of the lumber companies and had been there all winter while we had stayed with Grandmother.

I was four and a half, and brother Lex was two and a half. It was the first time we had seen a boat or a large body of water. I loved it at once. We stood on deck by the rail and watched the water as it danced and sparkled in the sunlight and the white gulls flying in a blue sky.

We wanted to see everything, and Mother took us through the boat to the stern, and around to the side to watch the wheels. We peeked down stairways, into passages, and finally sat down in a sheltered place.

As the boat headed north across the open waters of the bay, the wind stiffened, and soon it was so rough that we had to go into the saloon where it was warm and stuffy and smelled of oil and other things and made us all feel sickish. Mother fixed a place for me to lie down on a wide cushioned seat that ran along either side under the windows. I was not really sick, but did not care to move, so lay very quiet all afternoon listening to the engine throbbing, the waves roaring and the great wheels on either side plunging into them. The boat rolled from side to side. The windows on the opposite side went up and down — up, and I could see nothing but sky; down, and I could see nothing but dark blue water -– greenish-blue. It would poise a moment and repeat. This went on and on until I fell asleep and did not know when we entered the shelter of the islands and the sun went down.

It was dark when we passed through the channel, around the island into the harbor, and tied up at the dock.

When I awoke, I was in my Father's arms. He was carrying me down the gangplank, with Mother carrying Brother beside us. Through the darkness we drove to the little house that was to be our home.

From Galt to Parry Sound

We had come from a beautiful farming country, the "Garden of Ontario", where there were fields of grain, fat sleek-looking cattle, fine horses in stables, great bank barns, lofts filled with hay in which the hens laid eggs, bins of oats and corn, where fruits of all kinds matured and ripened, and berries, currants, and vegetables were abundant, where fine, prosperous little cities and villages were quite close to each other and connected by good roads and railroads. A land of plenty.

The country we had come to live in was wild and beautiful. It looked as though there had been a mighty upheaval in past ages, when the rocks were split and torn asunder and scattered far and wide. The glaciers must then have passed over, smoothing and rounding the rocks, filling the cracks and hollows with debris, and then receding, leaving only bare, low hills of rock, their tops ground off smooth and barren.

In the deep hollow to the south, a great lake had formed, and all along its shore, thousands of islands were strewn — some mere rocks sticking up out of the water, some large islands miles long and wide.

Halfway along the shore, a fine harbor had formed, sheltered behind the island, a protection from storm. The harbor pushed its way inland to meet a river, rippling down the valley from the hills above and forming rapids as it joined the waters of the harbor.

The islands and the mainland were thickly wooded

over large tracts with all the hardy northern trees: white and red pine, spruce, ash, maple, beech, birch, cedar, oak, walnut, and tamarack, and the grey rocks stuck out everywhere.

The "bush" teemed with animal life. The graceful deer, the clumsy bear, the hungry wolf, the sly fox, the muskrat, the skunk, the porcupine, the rabbit, and the squirrel lived in it and came down to the river in the valley to drink with the industrious beaver and the otter. On its rocks the copperhead and rattler sunned themselves, partridges drummed in the heart of it, birds filled it with their beauty and song, honking geese and ducks flew over it, and many stayed all summer in this secluded spot.

The waters were full of fish.

Wild berries were thick in their season.

It was a "happy hunting ground" for the Indians. Besides food in abundance, and skins for their wigwams and clothing, there was plenty of birch bark for their canoes, cedar for the frame work, fibrous roots of tamarack "to bind the ends together", resin "to close the seams together", and quills "to deck her bosom."

Their village on the river and around the inner harbor was protected from the cold north winds in winter by the hills and forests that surrounded them on the north, east, and west, and from storms and enemies from the south in summer by the islands. It was a well known stopping and trading center. Here the Indians gathered from all the villages up and down the shore and along the rivers, coming in their long birch canoes to trade and barter, to dance their weird and solemn dances, and to smoke the Peace Pipe together.

If you have read Hiawatha, it is easy to imagine their daily lives, and — down to fundamentals — they were not unlike our own. They had the same problems and cares, sorrows and joys, loves and jealousies, in a different setting.

The women had their children to care for, the cooking to do, dressmaking, embroidering, basket weaving, and "wigwam-keeping". They were quiet, attending to their home duties with apparently no though of a career, yet they seem to have had quite as much influence in their tribe councils as the new woman of today has in our government.

The men protected the village from enemies, made canoes and fishing and hunting outfits, brought in the food, attended to the business of trade and barter, and all outside affairs.

They all went on long trips together in their great canoes to visit their friends in other villages, to pick berries on the islands, and to hunt and fish in and out among them.

Near their wigwams they planted maize, and before it — with the papoose strapped to a back cradle (dick-e-nag in Ojibwa), snug and warm and leaning up against a tree, smiling good-naturedly — I have seen the squaws cooking, making moccasins and clothes for winter, fancy and useful baskets and sleighs and snowshoes, embroidering with quills and beads, and tanning furs.

The Indians

The Indians must have been surprised when they saw the first white men — trappers or Jesuits, probably, soon to be followed by explorers and lumbermen.

The white men won the friendship of the Indians first with soft words and gifts. They traded with them, but paid them mostly with trash. They took their lands and forests in the name of the King, and in their masterful way they endeavored to impose their civilization and a new and bewildering religion upon them. It was a long, long way to the seat of Authority, but in time adjustments were made and laws were passed. The white man took legal possession of all the land except certain reservations that were given to the Indians with certain rights and privileges and a small money payment to be made quarterly to each one.

How much they were paid for their inheritance, how much persuasion or force was necessary to make them finally give up in this region, I do not know. When we arrived, the Indians were on the big island to the south, which was ten or twelve miles long and half as wide, called the Indian Reservation. There they lived, a quiet subdued people, some still pagan, some Catholic, and some Methodist, but mostly living their own lives regardless of civilization.

A few small houses, a Methodist Church, and a school house had been built on their island. They were friendly and law-abiding except when crazed with liquor, which was not often as it was a serious offense to sell or give an Indian liquor.

They came to the village only to sell their fish, berries, and baskets, and to buy provisions, crossing during the open season in fleets of canoes, and in winter on the ice, walking single file, drawing large cedar sleighs piled high with their produce. There were moccasins of deer skin that wrapped around the ankle and tied with thongs, the vamps decorated with beads or quills, baskets for laundry and market, snowshoes and sleighs, fancy baskets and mats, and small canoes, all for the souvenir trade, and fish that they caught through a hole in the ice. They sold from house to house or traded at the stores where they stood around the stove enjoying the warmth and filling the place with their smoky buckskin odor. Then finally, the business of the day completed, their sleighs loaded, the sun lowering in the west, they would start out again on the long walk across the ice to their island home.

When the Jesuits first saw the Hurons, they were a proud people — confident and capable. Twenty five years later, they were a pitiable remnant. The Hurons blamed the "Black Robes" for their misfortunes: "It is the priest that kills us. Before he came we were happy and prosperous. He has bewitched the country."

Mrs. Jamison, an English lady, visited Mackinac in 1837. In a book she wrote about it, she says of the Indians, "The propinquity of the white man is destruction to the red man. The further the Indians are removed from us, the better for them. In their own woods — a noble race. Brought near to us — a degraded and stupid race. We are destroying him."

My First Day in Parry Sound

When the sun woke me next morning, I was in a small bare room with nothing in it but two little beds. Lex was asleep in the other one. Through a doorway I could see another bed, but it was empty. Then I heard talking and recognized Mother's voice, so I slid out of bed and started on an adventure through that strange house to find her.

Out in the hall there was a stairway that was quite dark at the bottom, but I trusted that there was a door. Down I crept, and with a gentle push the door opened, and there was a large sunny room with furniture and trunks standing 'round. There was also a smell of breakfast from a room to the side, and when I looked in, there was Mother waving to someone at an open door. I rushed over and grabbed her — so glad to see her — and then I looked out to see whom she was waving at. It was Father going through a gate at the end of a long path from the house.

I asked, "Where is Father going, Mother?"

She said, "To the mill."

I remember about the mill. Father had always had to get up early and go to the mill to work every day except Sundays to earn money to buy food and clothing and all the other things needful for all of us. Mother had often told us about that so I did not have to ask why, but took Mother's hand, and we went around to look at everything, until we heard Brother calling from upstairs. Up we went to get him, and I dressed myself.

While we were eating breakfast, a bell rang, and Mother said, "That must be the school bell. That is the school house across the road." I ran to the door, and there were a lot of children playing in the school yard, and making such a nice noise laughing and shouting. More and more children came, but soon the bell rang again, and they all went in the door, and all was quiet.

Father came home for dinner, and when he went back to the mill I walked with him to the gate and stood there watching him until he turned a corner and was out of sight. I ran to the corner to see him again, and to see what it looked like down the street. Yes, there was Father walking very fast, but there was no mill in sight. I stood there a long time just looking. All around that corner was a white picket fence, and behind it a fine looking house with a veranda around two sides of it and a lawn with trees and vines and flowers. Across the street there was a long, plain, one story building, painted white, and with broad steps leading up to a wide door. It was at the foot of a hill which rose gradually at the side of it to quite a height, at the top of which was a kind of tower. The sandy road rounded the corner at the foot of the hill, the main road going north past our house, but a branch turned off to the left over a low rise, past the south end of the school, the sandiest road I had ever seen. Beyond the school was a church with a steeple and bell. And there was Mother calling me.

The House

Our plain, awkward little house had no style and no conveniences, but it was not long before it began to look homelike and comfortable. Mother had a gift that way. The furniture was ordinary, and there was no more of it than was necessary, so it was not cluttered. The windows were full of flowering plants, ferns, and ivies. There were geraniums of all colors, chrysanthemums, begonias, foliage plants, fuchsias loaded with blossoms, and most of the old fashioned house plants. All winter long Mother kept them from freezing. During a severe cold spell, every one of them had to be moved to a warmer place, where they would stay sometimes for days. Seldom were they frozen, and how we did appreciate them when they were all in the windows again!

Outside also, the place was redeemed by Mother's flowers. The house was set far back on the lot, so that instead of a lawn in front there was a vegetable garden, which was a necessity, as each one had to grow most of his own. Father took charge of that, but he left a wide border along the path on either side and in front of the house for flowers. There Mother planted all the slips and seeds she could get, exchanging hers with all her friends and neighbors. She always accompanied her callers to the gate in pleasant weather, and they seldom went away without some little offering: a flower, a slip, or a few seeds. When she called on them, she was sure to return home with a handful of treasures.

In the early morning, after Father went to the mill, and before we children were up, she loved to work out among them. Often I ran along the path to her in an ecstasy of delight over the loveliness of the morning and my young and pretty mother.

Sunday

On Sundays, Father did not go to the mill, and we all slept later. On Saturday nights we all had very thorough hot baths, clean nighties and bed linen, shoes were polished, and our Sunday clothes laid out ready to put on. How happy and "good" I always felt as I said my prayer and cuddled down in my clean, warm bed.

I loved Sunday morning. The church bells rang out. The Episcopal Church across the street mingled its chimes with those of the Methodist Church, and we timed ourselves by them, as our church had no bell. Before the last bell rang out, we were on our way down the street to the corner and across to the plain, white building with the broad steps, which turned out to be the Presbyterian Church to which Father belonged.

Inside it was plain, also — as plain as could be. There was a low platform at the end opposite the door, with an organ and chairs for the choir, and on an extension in the center, a pulpit and three comfortable chairs. The rest of the room was filled with good wooden pews, lacking cushions and foot stools. It was heated by a large box stove which stood in a space reserved for it at the end of the seats on one side.

We had a pew of our own, as did all the members. The four of us sat in that pew for years, joined every two or three years by another member, until there were ten of us. We sat there together every Sunday morning and evening, until some of us went up to sing in the choir.

Sunday

The minister that first morning was of the old school, with a clerical collar and long black coat. He was very solemn looking, and when he paid his first call upon us, I was, for once, speechless. He did not smile, but read a chapter in the Bible, prayed, and with a few appropriate words, departed. Poor man: he did not stay long, and was the last of his kind in our church.

Captain Skene

When I awoke on those mornings when Mother was out in her flower garden, I would run down the path to her. An elderly gentleman, out for an early "constitutional", passed every morning, usually with just a nod and a touch of his hat, but when we were near the gate, he would stop and chat a while.

He was Captain Skene, a retired army captain from Scotland, acting at that time as Indian Agent, and living in a red brick house at the end of our street. He had a housekeeper, who soon called on Mother and invited me to the Captain's birthday party. He liked little girls, she said, and she invited a dozen or more every year to celebrate his birthday. There were games and prizes, and a large cake, in the depths of which were buried a ring, a thimble, and a ten-cent piece. The lucky finder of the ten-cent piece was to be the Captain's "wife" for a year.

Once I was the lucky finder. When I went to pay my "duty call" – which was the only "duty" required, it was a formal occasion. I was dressed up in my best, walked up to the front door, and rang the bell. I was admitted and shown into the library where the Captain was sitting. He would rise, shake hands, and place a chair for me, as though I were a grown up lady. It was a most attractive room. There was a bay window full of flowers, and a side window before which stood a fernery, glass covered and all green and dewy inside; on the table a bowl of huge pansies or other flowers, and the whole room redolent of flowers and tobacco.

When we were comfortably seated — he in his big leather chair with wide leather straps hooked over brass knobs for arms — he would take off the lid of a lovely creamy-white jar, and say, "Shall we smoke?" Passing the jar to me I would help myself to a stick of twisted creamy-white candy, and then he would light his pipe.

We would "smoke" and visit pleasantly until the candy was all gone, and then I would rise and say, "I must be going."

The Captain enjoyed it all from a dignified distance, but it was his friend and housekeeper whom we should have thanked for our happy times. She it was who went to all the bother of planning and cake-making, in an effort to brighten the lives of a lonely old man and a few little girls.

The Tugboat Trip

Captain Burrett, of the tug Mittigrew, invited us to go with him and his wife on a trip up the shore to get their daughter, Eleanor, who was teaching at Carling, a country school. Father took us down at noon on maple-shaded James Street to the dock where the tug was tied up. It was a perfect summer day – not a ripple on the water except the swell as it spread out fan-shaped behind her. We stood on deck and really saw the Harbor for the first time. To the north were the long lines of lumber piles and the mill where Father worked, the hills rising behind them and all around the shore; to the south, the grey-green Islands.

We went through the Channel into the Sound, toward the west, the smooth swell of our little boat radiating to the farthest corners and washing up on the shore. We sailed along in the warm sunshine, the engine throbbing, a gentle breeze blowing, for a long time, and then came up to a crude landing in a shady nook. Ashore, we children played around under the trees and on the pebbly shore where the clear water sparkled and lapped softly, but we did not have long to wait for our attractive passenger. "All aboard!" and the tug backed out into the sunshine again, turned in a long curve, and headed toward home.

We went again for Eleanor Burrett that summer in Mr. Arthur Starkey's large sailboat. There was a stiff breeze blowing, and the water was rough. The wind filled her big sails, and she dipped alarmingly,

77

sometimes taking in water, but when I saw that the men were not afraid and that she always righted herself, I began to enjoy it and ever since have wanted to get as near to the water as possible without getting drenched. Instead of going straight ahead, she tacked from one side to the other, but finally did make the landing in the shady nook. It was a gloriously thrilling trip.

The General Store

The main street in our town – Seguin Street – ran in a gentle slope from our corner to the river, crossing James Street half way. It was not long before I was trusted to go down this street almost to the bridge to the Company's store for small purchases. It was a general country store, with dry goods on one side and groceries on the other. At the back were boots and shoes, stoves and hardware, dishes and lamps, and many other necessities. Beyond was the big storehouse filled with bales and boxes, barrels of sugar and molasses, flour and feed, coal oil, paint, and "what-not". There was a big scale on which to weigh everything, including little girls, and through the large unloading door the morning sun streamed.

I was most interested in the grocery department. There was a big red coffee mill in which the clerk, Robert Spring, ground our coffee. He would talk to me all the time he was grinding, and sometimes let me try. Overhead hung a large picture of Queen Victoria in full regalia in colors. But the main attraction was a showcase in which candy was displayed. I waited there while the clerk wrote in the little black book I always brought with me, and passed it through a tiny door in the wall just below Queen Victoria into the office. In a moment it was passed back, and when Mr. Spring brought it and my parcel to me, he usually slipped his hand into the showcase and brought forth a candy, which he gave to me. I surely hadn't asked for it; no, that would not be polite, and I do hope I never forgot to say "thank you."

The Mill

The Water Mill, run by water power, where Father worked, was on the river, a block or two south of the bridge. It was raised ten or twelve feet above the ground and was surrounded on three sides by a tramway. This elevated tramway branched out on either side of the river, on the west side extending to the docks and on the east crossing above the dam and running along the shore of the harbor for several hundred feet.

On both sides of these tramways, the lumber was piled in double rows, ten or twelve feet above them. It was brought from the mill on horse-drawn cars and piled systematically with air spaces between. The lumber vessels were tied up along side to be loaded.

Father was the Culler and Shipper. Tanned and powdered with sawdust, in his hand a flexible yardstick with a handle at one end and a brass hook to turn the boards on the other, he supervised a gang of men who carried the lumber onto the boat and passed it to others who stowed it in the hold until it was piled above the decks.

All summer long the vessels and sailing ships were being loaded at the different yards, a dozen or more at a time. They went out usually bound for ports in the United States: Bay City, Detroit, Buffalo, Tonawanda were familiar names to us.

The river was divided by a floating plank walk, from the upper rapids above the bridge to the dam.

The logs coming down on the west side of it were for the Water Mill. Those on the other side belonged to the two big steam mills on the harbor. They had to go down a sluice-way, and usually there was a "river driver" or two to direct the logs and keep them moving. The tramway, for a short distance over the dam, was a shortcut, and when we went that way, we would stop to watch the logs go down and listen to the men talking and laughing together.

They were rather picturesque in their tall, broad-brimmed hats and their red woollen scarves wound twice around their waists and tied in a knot at the hips, with two tasseled ends. They wore great spiked boots and carried long pike poles. When the river was full of logs, these men were on all night working by the light of the moon or lanterns. We would stop on the bridge to listen to them talking, laughing, and often singing softly as they walked around on the moving, dipping logs as nonchalantly as though they were on terra firma.

There were times during the spring break-up when the work was strenuous and more or less dangerous, when they struggled and used strong language in the effort to keep the logs from jamming.

The Saw

Walking up the ramp to the tramway on the north side of the Mill, through a large doorway could be seen the shining circular saw. The wet logs were directed onto the carrier, which brought them up into the mill to meet the saw that transformed them into lumber. It sparkled, buzzed, and whined shrilly as the carriage brought the log to it, and it ripped through. Back and forth went the carriage, the log turned each time by a cant hook until slabs were cut off the four sides, and the square timber cut into one inch boards.

One day as I stood watching it, the man on the carriage asked me if I would like to have a ride. Of course, I accepted and stepped on beside him. It was a little frightening to be so near the saw and to think what might happen . . . but I saw the whole log through, glad I had done it, but not anxious to do it again.

There is a great deal of wastage in slabs and sawdust. The people of the village carted away great loads of slabs to be used for kindling and summer stove wood. Sawdust and slabs were also used for filling in and building up roads and low places. There was still so much of it that the company had to erect a huge, tall burner, screened at the top, into which the refuse was conveyed by a chain carrier, and burned night and day all the season. Each of the little mills had a burner, and the red glare from them at night helped to brighten up a village that was not well lighted.

Fire!

The Water Mill had a bell, the Steam Mills had whistles, and they rang and whistled four times a day, except on Sundays. When there was a fire anywhere in town, the bell tolled insistently, and the whistles tooted compellingly, arousing the whole population, especially at night. Everyone who could walk was there as soon as the volunteer fire brigade.

It was a serious matter if a mill was on fire, and a sight worth seeing. The wooden structures and lumber in flames, with barrels of oil going up like rockets, one after the other, made a terrible but thrilling sight for those of us who knew nothing of fireworks. The women and children would gather on the hillside wrapped in anything warm they could lay their hands on quickly, while the men went to work with the firemen. It would be as light as day all around, the flames reflected in the water. As they increased, the excitement was intense, and as they faded, thoughts of the future filled everyone's mind. It upset everything for the rest of the season usually, and no man knew what kind of a job he would have, or if he would have any.

School

When school began about September first, in the little school house across the street from us, I was a beginner and sat in the front row with another little girl. It was very exciting sitting there with all the other children and a much-admired teacher. My dress was new, and I carried a slate, slate pencil, and book.

There were only two rooms, with a hall and cloak rooms between. In one room, the younger half of the pupils were taught by a young woman, and in the other, the older pupils were under a "master", who was Head or Principal. He was a Scot, always called the "Dominie", who always carried a stick, which he used as a pointer and for other purposes.

Reading, 'riting, and 'rithmetic were taught quite thoroughly, as we realize now, taking in their stride spelling, literature, history, geography, and all the branches that are now subjects. Grammar came in the higher classes. Many poems and literary gems had to be memorized, are still remembered, and enjoyed much more now that they were then.

On Friday afternoons, after recess, instead of regular work, we had an hour of entertainment: a spelling match or a geography match, with readings, recitations, and singing.

Outdoors we played all the games known to children: tag, baseball, crack-the-whip, London Bridge, anti-over, prisoner's base, hide-and-seek, and, of course, marbles, jacks, and skipping. No equipment was provided by the school and none was expected or seemed necessary. But there were no children standing around doing nothing during recess.

Some of the older girls played house. They took the stones that were everywhere and laid out rooms, kitchen, dining room, bedroom, and parlor, and were much concerned about their housekeeping and family cares. They "called" on each other and discussed their problems as housewives have ever done. Each had a "child" chosen from among the smallest pupils, and as I was small, I was in demand. They were having such fun that they began staying after school to play, and asked me to wait for them at the schoolroom door, as the lower classes were always out first, while in the other room they were still standing before a map having a geography lesson. The door opened a bit, a hand appeared, and drew me into the room behind the taller girls. The map, and what the Dominie was saying, interested me at once, and all would have gone well if the girls had been attentive. He soon realized that something distracting was going on, however, and when the cause was discovered, I was hustled out, bursting with hurt pride and resentment. I went straight home, leaving the girls without a "child".

In time a much larger school was built in another part of town which we all attended for years, but it is the little old school house and what we learned there that pops into my mind almost every day — the Seat of Learning to me.

The Seasons – Fall

When the feel of Autumn is in the air, and the grass and small shrubs are yellow and dried, the grey rocks stand out bare and unrelieved, except for the trees, which seem to have faded also. Then a wonderful change takes place. They are given a new lease of life and beauty. The maples and sumacs turn to brilliant reds and yellows, the oak leaves turn a darker reddish brown, and all the other trees take on many shades of yellow, red, and brown, with a background of dark evergreens. Yellow goldenrod, purple asters, and brown cattails in the lower moist places form a mass of vivid color that only the home folks are there to enjoy usually.

Indian summer, a few perfect hazy days in October, air like champagne, water sparkling in the sunlight, and trees gorgeously colored, made an impressive and cheery "au revoir" to summer.

The colors faded, and the wind blew the leaves off the trees and scattered them far and wide over the earth to nourish it and enable it to bring forth more needful and beautiful gifts when the winter was over. Frost came and hardened the earth, snow fell and laid a warm white covering over all, and the little roots and seeds, insects, and bears were tucked in warm and safe for the long winter rest.

September was fall-like. Equinoctial gales blew in around the twenty-first. We watched the weather anxiously on account of the boats on the lakes. In church we sang often a prayer "For Those in Peril on the Sea." When the wind howled the loudest, we walked over the Hill to the Bluff to see the waves come in and dash wildly on that rocky shore, and thought of the sailor men being buffeted by them.

October came in calm and beautiful, with sunny days and frosty nights. The maple trees were a mass of brilliant reds, and all the other trees were putting on their lovely autumn colors with the dark green pines a somber background. There was the glorious time called Indian Summer, when the sun during the day was warm and hazy and the air was soft with the sweet, earthy aroma.

During September and October there were many days when we could play outdoors, but toward the end of November the winter weather really began. The sun rose late and it was dark early, so our day was short. After school I stayed indoors and played with my brother. Mother told us stories about real people mostly, instead of fairies and ogres, and the one we liked best was about ourselves. We asked for that story nearly every day, and patiently Mother repeated it over and over again. When it snowed, we stood at the window and watched the snowflakes falling, or when the panes were frosted, blew holes so we could see out.

Mother was busy making woolen dresses, coats, and underwear. There were caps, tam-o-shanters, scarves, and mittens to be knitted or crocheted, and it was not long before I was doing my share of it. There was also the fall house-cleaning and the work of preparing it for the winter. Those who could afford it had double windows and extra porches on outside doors. Those who could not afford these luxuries tightened up the windows, filled the cracks and crevices with paper and strips of cloth, put lath wound with cloth around the doors, banked the foundation with sand and sawdust, and battened down the whole place for zero weather.

The cellars were stocked with barrels of potatoes, apples, vegetables, cases of eggs packed in salt, and hams. The shelves were filled with canned fruit, pickles, chili sauce, catsup, jelly, raspberry vinegar "for occasions", and everything we could gather that would help out our diet during the long winter ahead.

The wood shed was piled high with sweet-smelling hard wood and pine for kindling, and stoves were put up with much fussing over ill-fitting stove pipe.

Stores also were filled to capacity with the long list of necessities and the few luxuries that it was estimated would be enough to carry us over until Spring.

And if our preparations and canning and setting by and stocking up were not enough for the winter, we could begin to run out of necessities before Spring. Once it was coal oil. The stage brought a little for certain persons, but the village as a whole was reduced to candle and firelight. Another time it was flour and potatoes, and you can imagine how eager we were to see the first boat that Spring.

November brought more cold and snow and a spell of stormy weather. The last boat came in toward the end of the month, and when she departed, the village was almost completely cut off from the outside world. All that we knew of what was going on came through the newspapers and letters from friends.

Most of the men who had worked in the mills during the summer went to the logging camps in the "bush" for the winter, and came out only once during that time. They were paid and given a few days off for Christmas so that the married men could be with their families and the younger men could "let off steam" a little by celebrating. Professional men — educators, ministers, store keepers, office men — were left in town to look after things. Father was one of these as he worked in the Company office while the Mill was closed.

The Loss of the Waubuno

Our small passenger boat, the Waubuno, the same little side-wheeler that had brought us to this North Shore, was expected on her last trip of the season. The weather was very stormy and great anxiety was felt for her safety. Night came on, snow falling heavily, wind howling, and still no sign of her.

Early in the morning a man came to our door and told Father that she had not arrived. They were getting up a party to go in search of her and asked him to go with them. Dressed in his warmest clothes, he hurried out into the dark storm, and did not return until late that night. They had not found one trace of her. Later, when the wind and waves had calmed down, wreckage appeared, and she was located in deep water, apparently having capsized, going completely over and holding all on board inside, so that not one body was recovered.

It was a great shock to the whole community. We all loved the little boat that had served us so well, and meant so much to each one. We knew the men, too, and mourned for them. Captain Campbell's wife and others made a desperate effort to have her raised and the bodies recovered, but nothing could be done until Spring, and in the end it was never done. The Captain's wife and little girl came to our place several times to talk to Father about it. They were both dressed in deep mourning. It seemed very sad to me to see such a little girl in black.

A loud cry went up against the Steamship Companies, who risk the lives of their men by sending them out in treacherous weather when the chances are great that they will never make port. All for a few extra dollars. One of the old captains — Captain McQuade — who had sailed the lake most of his life, quoted the words, "Man's inhumanity to man . . .", which is still the most disheartening thing in life.

Winter

The clean white snow, good sleighing, and moderate temperature of December made it a pleasant month — the night almost as light as day with the moonlight shining on the snow. On clear nights when there was no moon, the snow relieved the darkness, and the stars sparkled like diamonds in the sky. When the clouds hung heavy, the long evenings around our big dining room table — with the children studying and doing homework, Mother mending or making button holes, Father reading the paper, a bowl of apples, the room warm and cozy — were times one can never forget. The children in bed, Mother would read for a while.

We began to hear much about Christmas and Santa Claus, and promises were made that if we were good children, he would bring us certain things we wished for. I often sat up with Mother making gifts for the other children. It was all a great secret and could not be done during the day.

The stores advertised and decorated very little, but inside they displayed quite a large and varied stock of Christmas goods. At school someone recited "Twas the Night Before Christmas" or read "The Christmas Carol", and at Sunday School the lessons were about the birth of Christ. We sang "Hark the Herald Angels Sing", "O Little Town of Bethlehem", and "Holy Night". Trees and entertainments at Sunday School came during the holiday week.

But Santa Claus and Christmas trees did not appear anywhere until Christmas Eve or Christmas morning. We were then in a state of great expectation and excitement, and were awake in the morning long before dawn, shivering with cold and excitement. Our parents, tired and sleepy after working late the night before, but cheerful with the Christmas spirit, wrapped us up and took us down to the warm living room, dimly lit by the firelight from the big stove through its mica windows. We could smell the tree and the oranges, and the suspense was great until the lamps were lit and we could really see the feast Santa had prepared for us: toys, books, clothes, candy, red apples, nuts, and little cakes.

Father stayed home most of the day, played ninepins with us and looked at our new picture books. Mother was busy as only a mother can be, with little time for rest or play until dinner was over.

The Episcopalians had several services during the morning. The Church was decorated with evergreens made into long "chains" which were wreathed around pillars and outlined the altar, windows, and doors, and there was much good music. We attended sometimes when we could tear ourselves away from our home festivities.

In the late afternoon of that first Christmas in Parry Sound, it began to snow. We were tired and drowsy, perhaps a little lonely, when there was a knock at our door, and there was our neighbor's son, Rob, with an invitation to spend the evening with them. A shawl was wrapped around me and he carried me over to his house in the falling snow. Mother and Father soon followed with Brother and tiny baby sister, Colene.

Our neighbor's, the McClellands, home seemed very large and grand, with every room lighted as brightly as coal oil lamps could light them. There was a tree and many gifts to look at. Bowls of fruit, nuts, and raisins, and candy stood around temptingly. There was a fascinating kaleidoscope, and a stereoscope with a large box of views, which Rob's little sister, May, showed me, and so many other things that I could not see enough that night, so was invited to come again, which I did many times that winter.

There was much sociability during the week, entertaining for those home for the holidays, and outdoor sports if the weatherman was kind, which he was, nearly always. On New Year's Day the ladies received the gentlemen of their acquaintance at their homes. They came alone or in groups all day, and were served with refreshments. In the evenings there were small parties and sometimes a large "assembly".

The weatherman, conscious of good behavior for so long, could stand the repression no longer and would burst out in a fury of storm and cold for a week or two, and then as if exhausted or sorry, would bring on a "soft spell" called January thaw, when the sun was warm and the snow melted a little.

Blizzard!

The January thaw was usually followed by a drop in temperature as low as 40 degrees below zero, and staging, in the end, a howling blizzard in February. The roads would be blocked and the small houses almost buried in snow. The snow was hard like specks of ice or steel, and the wind whirled it into huge drifts, obliterating fences, paths, and roads. No school, business at a standstill, living in one or two rooms with fires bright and hot, lamps lighted – it was fun if it did not last too long.

At first let-up, the boys and men, in warm fur or woollen caps drawn well over forehead and ears, lumber jackets, shoepacs, mufflers, and mittens, would be out with snow shovels, working like beavers, making paths and clearing roadways, shouting to each other, laughing and thoroughly enjoying themselves. Crude, horse-drawn snow ploughs working on the streets, the horses as glad as the men to be out again, and soon the sleighs and big cadge teams would be jingling up and down them, doing business as usual, the sun shining, life normal once more.

Though dry, it was cold, no doubt about it. The northwest wind that met us on the hilltops on our way to school was piercing and seemed to freeze our very eyelashes, which was about all of us that was left uncovered on such days. Coat collars were turned up and held tight by a woollen scarf wound over caps, round the head and neck up to the eyes, through which the breath came like steam out of a teakettle and freezing it stiff. Sometimes cheeks were frozen, and care had to be taken to thaw them out before going near the fire, as it is very painful if thawed out too quickly. Frozen ears not properly cared for were forever after enlarged, floppy, and sensitive. Fingers and toes tingled, and we would have to clap our hands and stamp our feet to aid circulation and warm them up a little before going near the stove to avoid chilblains.

Storms and Arctic weather were only occasional. We took them as a matter of course, and the worse they were, the more we enjoyed telling about it later.

There was much lovely weather, and winter brought many compensations. That a snow- and ice-clad landscape can be beautiful is surely proven by the number of times it is chosen as a subject by artists and photographers, and admired and loved by many who have to put up with hardship and inconvenience on account of it. A sparkling day, a brilliant night, or one gorgeous with Northern Lights streaming out of a hazy northern cloud, shimmering southward with a soft sound like rustling silk, spreading fanlike in sheets of silver, rose, yellow, and bluish green — their mystic beauty thrills.

There is nothing gayer than sleigh bells, and they were heard everywhere in different tones, and what is so dashing and "swell" as a luxurious Russian sleigh, drawn by a team of fine horses and filled with warm fur robes. There was only one like that in town, but we enjoyed any kind, even the empty cadge teams that we could jump on behind if the driver was good-natured. Most of us walked wherever we went, no matter what the distance or the weather — if we went at all.

Winter Sports

Skating, with its games and carnivals, was probably the most popular sport. There were outdoor skating rinks at first. A large square was cleared of snow, which was heaped up on all four sides. It had to be flooded every night and kept clear of snow. A little pine shanty was put up near the entrance, in which there was a red hot stove that melted the sap in the boards, where skates could be put on in comfort. A bench outside accommodated the quicker, hardier skaters. It was lighted with torches at night, and the enterprising, hard-working young man who ran it was repaid by the sale of season tickets. Round and round we skated, sometimes together with crossed hands, or alone cutting figure eights, skating backwards, and other fancy stunts.

There were games of "shinny" or "curling" and, several times a season, a "carnival" when no one was allowed on the ice who was not in costume.

As one of the boys tells it: "Hockey was unknown, but the good old game of 'shinny' flourished mightily. All the men and boys on the lake who wished to play went into one game, with the goals perhaps a quarter of a mile apart; the puck: a block of wood, and the sticks: saplings with bent ends cut from the nearby woods. There was a goalkeeper on each side, and all the other players occupied the position of 'center forward'. If fifty were in the game, two kept the goals, and the other forty-eight scrimmaged for the puck, twenty-four on each side. If one fortunate or skillful player secured the puck and made a dash for the distant goal, there was a wild chase to intercept him, and much yelling. If he had speed and luck, he would secure a shot on the goal with only the goalkeeper to say him 'nay'. So the sport went on until the small boys could hardly drag themselves home, but they were at it again next day as hard as ever. Usually snow fell all too soon and put an end to the fun."

Deep in the woods was a little lake, a mile or so from the village. In summer the road to it was a favorite walk for lovers and friends; in winter, when there was good skating on the lake, it was alive with boys, men, and young people, hurrying along with clanking skates over their shoulders. There they skated for hours, round and round, in winter sunshine or moonlight.

In time the "rink" became a large wooden structure, with warm rooms at the entrance and benches all around for spectators and resting. There we saw many a stirring game of hockey (no longer called "shinny") and "bonspiel" (curling tournament), and watched the gay and solemn and funny costumes glide by in the carnival.

But the skating we enjoyed the most was in the open on the Bay. When it froze over first, and the snow held off, it was a sheet of smooth ice which hardened up more every night until it was pronounced safe. Fortunately, it happened several times during Christmas week when the college boys were home and other holiday visitors were there. We skated morning and afternoon for hours at a time and went long distances down among the Islands. The ice would crack sometimes with a loud report and leave a space about a foot wide that had to be jumped. Groups would skate together sometimes in a long line holding hands. An ice boat or two was something new, but all the old stunts and games we enjoyed just as much. Toward the end of the week the ice would be pretty well cut up, then clouds would appear and snow would fall, covering it all with a clean white blanket.

Snowshoeing was strenuous, but fun. The moon shining brightly on the white snow, the crust hard enough to hold up, and with good company, it was a special event. Sometimes we broke through the crust, and there were fences to climb when we girls had to have assistance, but that was no hardship, and then to end the evening at someone's home feeling hungry and tired, being served delicious refreshments, and too tired to dance, and it's impossible to dance in moccasins anyway — a perfect ending to a happy evening.

The toboggan slide, running through high banks of snow for almost a mile, torch lights all along its course, the tobogganists in colorful costumes, was another winter gathering place. At the signal, the toboggan shot down the send-off, which was a sheet of glare ice, and sped away out of sight. Another toboggan was on the course in front, and one was due to start soon behind. If the one in front had a spill and did not get away in time, there was bound to be a mix up, and knowing that another followed added to the possibilities, but there were really few serious accidents, as there was careful timing and the men knew their toboggans. The long walk back to the send-off spoiled the fun for some folks, but mostly it was accepted as part of the sport, and riding back in horse-drawn sleighs was never even thought of.

Spring

Nearing Spring there was a period of intense cold — when the fires had to be kept burning full blast day and night and the woodpile dwindled rapidly — followed by a blizzard. Then the chilly winds of March and the showers and sunshine of April melted the snow and ice. Little rivulets trickled down the hillsides with gentle tinkling sounds that was music in our ears. The roads became wet and slushy, bare spots of earth appeared, on which the boys at once began to play marbles and the girls to skip, plants were set out in the rain, blankets and quilts were hung on the clothesline, and there was the smell and feel of Spring in the air.

We had to wear rubbers, and figured that with them on, it was quite all right for us to wade in the running water and puddles and to scuff through slush, becoming more daring every minute until it was over the tops of our rubbers and our feet soaking wet. The disgusted exclamation of "somebody" as we entered the house warned us that all was not well. Off came rubbers, shoes, and stockings, and they were hung up to dry. Warm dry stockings and slippers were put on, and we were not allowed to go out to play again that day – but it was worth it.

"Boat in Sight!"

Our year was divided into two seasons: the open season, when the waters were free of ice, and the closed season, approximately from December 1 to May 1, when they were frozen over and navigation was impossible.

By May first we were thoroughly tired of winter, and the first boat was longed for and looked for most intensely, as the end of winter and the beginning of a long delightful open season. If the boat was late in coming, someone was on the lookout most of the time, on top of the hill or on the bluff overlooking the Sound. Eyes were strained, searching for a dark speck with a tiny plume of white above it at the entrance, a distance of several miles, each one hoping to be the first to see her.

In school the quiet would be shattered by a boy (who must have played hookey) rushing in and shouting, "Boat in sight!" With one accord and without a word from the teacher, we were out the door and up the hill: no more school that day. There in plain sight could be seen the dark speck with the white plume above it, and we watched for a white puff of steam and listened for the faint whistle that should follow. On she would come until we could hear it plainly and, with a field glass, read the name on her bow and see the brass buttons on the Captain's coat.

As she entered the Harbor blowing her deep-toned whistle long and loud, a mighty cheer would go up from the crowd on the Hill, and it would turn as one and make for the docks to see her glide into port. Tied "fore and aft", the gangplank out, down would come the Captain with a wave of his hand, and there was a great welcome for him and all of his crew.

All ashore and the welcome over, the freight would begin to roll out, to replenish the store houses and cellars which were always nearly empty by that time.

The first boat was soon followed by other passenger and freight steamers and lumber vessels, some of them full-rigged sailing ships. The local fishing boats, tugs, and yachts were given general cleanups and fresh coats of paint.

The mills began to cut lumber, the bell of the Water Mill and the whistles of the Steam Mills, after months of silence, again regulated the days of the whole community. The sound of the saws, the clap of lumber being piled, the smell of sawdust, the red glare of the burners, were all harbingers of spring. It was still cold, and sometimes it was almost June before the trees were in leaf and the lilacs budding.

But why hurry a beautiful experience like Spring? It passes all too rapidly. Too soon the summer is over, the harvest ended, and Winter — also beautiful — has come again. Why do we not enjoy each day as it comes, instead of living in the future, wishing always for some other time, some other place, something other than we have?

Summer

The school did not close until the last week in June, only a few days before Dominion Day, July 1.

June was lovely: trees and grass brilliantly green, and the air warm, even hot at times, yet fresh and invigorating. Lilacs filled the air with their perfume, and the annuals and vegetables shot up remarkably fast.

Dominion Day with its sports and pink lemonade seemed to be accompanied always with a hot sun to usher in real summer weather. The speech making and sports were held in the Park, which was merely a cleared level space in the woods. It was surrounded on three sides by woods and on the north by a high bluff, and was pleasant on cool days, but breathless on a hot one. There were stands where cool drinks, fruit, candy, cigars, and all such things were sold, and many parties picnicked around the edge under the trees. Water events took place in the Harbor and were watched from the docks in the late afternoon. There were boat races, swimming races, log rolling, the climbing of the greasy pole, and much cheering from the crowd.

The river drivers contested in the log rolling. It was exciting when the log began spinning: the men with long poles in their hands, their feet moving rapidly, their bodies swaying, each trying to dislodge his opponent, and the final plunge into the water of one of them. The crowd would cheer, and the victor, breathing heavily but smiling happily, would wave his hand, step into a boat, and come ashore. The vanquished would also be picked up. He would come ashore dripping wet and good-naturedly shake hands with the winner.

The day ended with a torchlight procession of the boys and jokers of the town in grotesque costumes, called "Callithumpians".

The twelfth of July was Orangeman's Day. We were awakened early by the fife and drum, which was heard monotonously, off and on, all day. They marched through the streets in full regalia to a banquet in the town hall, and then dispersed for another year.

Boating

Real summer weather lasted for six or eight weeks. During August there were many visitors from "outside", and the Islands were full of campers. Many people owned islands and built camps on them to which they and their friends came every year. There were many college students, professors, and teachers returning home for their vacation, and almost every family had relatives and friends visiting them at one time or another.

There were lots of folks, and it was play time. There were picnics and fishing parties down among the Islands in launches and yachts, sailing parties in big boats with large, white sails, and little private affairs in catboats with room for two only. There were trips in pleasure yachts to more distant Islands where danced the lancers in the pavilion. As the yacht would plough her way home after dark, we would sit around on deck, singing or in silence, just as we felt. If it got too chilly, we would descend to the cabin or stand around the engine room door to enjoy its warmth.

The summer was not complete without at least one trip to the South Port on the daily passenger boat. It left the West dock at 6 a.m., took on passengers and freight at the East dock, and proceeded southward past the familiar nearby Islands, through the Narrows, weaving in and out, following carefully the deep water channel marked out on the charts, for half a day, coming only once out into the open waters of the bay around a mainland projection for a few miles. This was always the danger point in stormy weather.

Among the Islands the boat made several calls at landing places for the convenience of the campers. They were all there to meet the boat, some coming in canoes and rowboats, eager for mail and papers and provisions. They were a happy, jolly crowd, dressed in the prevailing "slacks", boasting of their catches, saying goodbye regretfully to one of their party, or greeting heartily a new arrival. They would stand there waving and shouting friendly nonsense until the ship was well under way, then disperse leisurely, some by water, some disappearing into the woods, and others into the little inns above the shore.

At noon the boat docked at the South Port, and there was the train, puffing and snorting, a rare sight for the natives from the North Shore. After a walk around town, they would return to their boat, which seemed almost like home, glad that they were going back on her for another lovely afternoon on the water.

It was pleasant to arrive at the home port in the evening, to see the familiar faces again, and to be met by special friends to whom you could tell all about the day, and hear what had gone on at home.

At this point, those living on the East side were welcome to come on board and ride over to the West dock where the boat tied up. It made an enjoyable, profitable evening. Young people of the East side talked to the Captain, the Purser, and other friends, rode over on the boat just as the sun was setting, met all the folks on the dock, walked through town, over the bridge, around the foot of the hill on the board walk and home again; and if a girl were fortunate enough to meet her boy friend, it was just grand — especially if there was a moon.

Canoes and Indians

The roads were rocky and sandy and up and down hills, so though it was "horse and buggy days", we seldom went driving. The roads were best in the winter when the snow made a smooth, even covering for several months. Our outings in the summer were all, or usually, on the water in all kinds of watercraft. Nearly every family had one of some kind. A few had beautiful cedar rowboats, light and well-finished in the natural color, with cushions and lazy-backs and rudders, which were carefully sheltered in boat houses. The Peterborough canoes, perfect in design and finish with wide smooth thwarts and cushions, were sheltered also and lifted out of the water when not in use. There were sailboats of all sizes, steam yachts and tugs, passenger and lumber carriers, and we went out on all of them at different times, and enjoyed each one for different reasons.

The canoe was a favorite. Canoeing is the poetry of motion, especially in the evening, gliding over the smooth water, hardly making a ripple or a sound. After the sun has gone down and the moon has risen, or on a bright, starlight night when stars are so clearly reflected in the water, it seems as though the canoe and its occupants are suspended between two heavens, and, looking over the side, as though one might fall into the depths of it. In a deep shadow, a phantom canoe passes noiselessly and disappears like a dream.

The canoe, however, is not merely a pleasure craft.

It is one of the most useful that we have and took a most important part in the opening up of this vast, wild country. The Indian birch bark canoe, which the discoverers found on their arrival, was soon adopted by them and used for transportation. Loaded with supplies, it carried them steadily and smoothly over the rough lakes, up the long rivers, into smaller creeks and waterways where larger craft were impossible, and landed the white man and his civilization hundreds of miles into the interior.

The Indians of the North Shore still use them daily for business purposes. From their Island Reservation they come to town to trade and barter, the canoes filled with their wares, and return with a load of provisions. In fleets of canoes, the men came in the morning to work in the lumber yards, loading boats when they needed "shu-nee-o". They insisted on being paid when the day's work was ended. When the six o'clock whistle blew they all came up to the office to get it, and the Company was never sure they would return in the morning, no matter how badly they were needed. One of them, their leader, proud of his ability to read and write, and of his knowledge of business ways, wrote one morning to Father:

> Dear Sir:
> I tell you today because me not come this morning. Me not much better. Me sick I don't next Monday may be better and tell you one man finded this morning he told me, that man, I come down before six o'clock morning, to me yesterday morning, Maybe catch cool,
> I am sir your friend Chief Peter Megis

When the fishing and hunting season were on, or the

berries ripe, they could not be hired. Off they would go, in search of happy hunting grounds in far channels and bays, where they could forget the white man and his strange ways, and be their own Indian selves for a while.

They were always friendly, and we were never afraid of them in any way. We went to their Island, into their homes, their school and their church. Father took me once to a "feast" there in celebration of some special occasion. They served bear, porcupine, venison, and roast beef. There were vegetables and fruit also, with cakes and pies for dessert, ending with speeches and sociability.

Some of the Indian boys attended our school when they reached the higher classes, and one of the girls went to a "ladies' college", but did not stay long enough for it to make much change in her.

The Indian women came in the Fall selling baskets, sleighs, and other things. They would come into the kitchen to warm themselves and Mother would give them a cup of tea or something and often buy mats and pretty baskets to send as Christmas gifts. We used Indian clothes baskets always, and usually had a sleigh or two.

The Islands

The Islands appeared greyish green in the deep blue waters surrounding them, with a background of brighter blue and fleeting white clouds sometimes, and at other times a dark ominous grey that blotted out most of the color and all of the sparkle. They were almost entirely of rock, the smaller ones showing green only in the center where a lone pine tree flourished with a few shrubs and a little grass wherever it was possible for it to grow, until the hot summer sun beat down upon it and burned it brown.

On the larger Islands, many trees grew, the dark pines towering above, with birch, spruce, maple, willow, and others in all shades of green, their white and brown trunks showing between. Sumac, berry bushes, vines, ferns, and mosses grew beneath in every possible place down to the water's edge, almost covering the rocky base in early summer. In the rich leaf mold, flowers grew to perfection and blossomed in season: violets, columbine, lady's slippers, lilies; in the wet places: flags, cattails, grasses; and on the surface of the water: white and yellow water lilies with green dragonflies hovering over them. Birds flitted around quietly in the shade during the hot summer, bumblebees buzzed from one flower to another gathering their store of honey, fish splashed in the water, and the canoeist paddling lazily in the shadow of the Island is calmed and rested by the harmony and beauty. He lives for a short time above the cares and sordid thoughts with which we waste so many valuable hours, in the rarified atmosphere of God's marvelous universe, and returns to everyday affairs refreshed and ready to tackle his problems with courage and hope. Though he slips back into low again, he never slips quite so far as before that short vacation among the Islands along the North Shore.

Camp Meeting

One week late in August, there was Camp Meeting. Founded by Rev. Allen Salt, an Indian Methodist missionary to the Indians of Georgian Bay, it was held annually for about thirty years. Our Methodist Church joined them in conducting the meetings, and all the other Churches of the village gave up their own services and attended also.

The Campground was a grassy level space at the foot of the bluff west of the Hill. The bluff was steep and rocky, but almost covered with trees, shrubs, ferns, moss, and all the little plants that love such a place. The woods surrounded it irregularly on the other three sides. The road to it was a very sandy one over a little rise, at the foot of which it turned south through a green, shady woods, fragrant with pine and leaf-mold. The trees arched overhead and underneath them grew wintergreen and partridge vines with their red berries.

But the path we liked best was over the Hill to the bluff overlooking the Sound. In time, there was a long flight of steps, but we loved the path, with steps formed of roots and rocks, that wound steeply to the sandy shore below and northward through the hazelnut bushes to the Campground.

At the end of this outdoor auditorium, there was a row of weathered buildings, the center one higher than the others, having a balcony or covered pulpit, where the leader and visiting ministers sat, protected from

112

sun and rain. Below was a large platform, where during the meetings there was an organ and chairs for a large choir. The small buildings on either side were used as shelters and camps, and were connected by high board fences with doors in them, thus forming a semi-circular enclosure.

In front of the speakers stand were three long rows of benches with an aisle dividing them. A few tall pines were left standing among the benches, giving shade during the day and at night supporting large lamps in glass cases. They were not sufficient, however, to illuminate the place, so at the four corners outside the benches, fireplaces were built. Raised eight or ten feet on four stout logs, shallow boxes filled with rock and sand were placed, and on these, fires were kept burning. There were steps around each one to enable the fire tenders to get the big chunks and logs in place. The four fires leaped and danced and added a weird, aboriginal touch to the rustic surroundings.

The Indians camped around the edges in tents and wigwams, the papoose snug and secure in his board cradle leaning against a tree, the other children playing around, the squaw cooking over an open fire, silent as a rule, but interested and friendly.

There were services every afternoon and evening for a week. Sunday morning service was formal, and afternoon meetings uneventful. But at night, with the fires burning, the pines sighing and moaning overhead, hearts seemed to be softened and emotions to over-run. The speakers were more ardent, the prayers longer and more pleading, the softly sung hymns more convincing, and many were moved to go up to the "altar" and cry for mercy. It was fascinating, yet fearful.

The last afternoon was a "farewell". Everyone stood up and formed two half circles which passed each other, all shaking hands and singing "God Be With You Til We Meet Again". Everyone had held the hand of everyone else. It seemed like a Holy Communion, and we parted feeling that there truly is brotherly love and fellowship in this world.

Fired!

When our baby, "Lottie", was about one year old, and we had lived in Parry Sound for five or six years, an election was called, probably for mayor. Among the candidates mentioned were Mr. Miller, president of the company, and Dr. Walton. Father went to Mr. Miller and asked him if he intended running for the office, and Mr. Miller said "No", so Father pledged his vote to Dr. Walton.

But Mr. Miller changed his mind and expected Father to vote for him regardless of his pledge to Dr. Walton. But Dad's word was as good as his bond, and he voted for Dr. Walton, who won.

Next morning, Dad was fired, to the surprise and indignation of everyone, including the employees of the Company. The office gave him a farewell and a beautiful gold locket for his watch chain, with his monogram on one side and engraved on the other: "Presented to F. R. Hogg by his friends in the Parry Sound Lumber Company."

Dad decided to "go West" to look for a new job.

The Move to Parry Harbor

We were all packed and ready to go aboard the "Magnettawan" at 2:30 a.m. soon after. I remember the friends coming in to say goodbye and the rush at the last moment, going out into the night and down James Street to the dock, where we saw the Magnettawan moving away, and realizing we were just five minutes too late. Next morning Dad walked in with a queer smile on his face, and said he had just accepted a position with the Midland and North Shore Lumber Company and, instead of going west, we would move over to Parry Harbor. He was to be bookkeeper and office manager, and the house was next door to the office.

We knew almost less about that part of town than we did about "out west", but the house pleased us. It was quite nice considering the time and place, with eight rooms, and a veranda both upstairs and down the full width of the house towards the Harbor. We really enjoyed those verandas and the rooms leading to them through French doors. There were green shutters on all the windows and the veranda doors. It was built right on the street with a closed porch over the front door.

On the lower veranda Dad put up a swing. I took care of the babies by the hour on that swing, singing to myself and the baby all the songs I liked, dreaming dreams and building castles in the air. On the upper veranda we kept track of all that was going on in the

116

harbor and across on the opposite shore. Dad had a good telescope. He kept it in a bureau drawer near the door, and with it we could see boats out in the Sound and their names, and when the first boat was expected someone kept watch most of the time.

We had a cute little melodeon in the parlor, and stiff lace curtains at the two windows, a center table with books and an album, and a "fancy" lamp, and some chairs and a horsehair sofa. In the hall in cold weather was a big heater and the stairway. In the living room was another stove and a big dining room table around which we sat in the evening studying our school work and doing our exercises. In summer the stoves were out for a short while, and there were more flowers in the room. On a hot day Colene loved to clean these rooms, and then adjust the shutters so that a cool, green light was over everything.

Parry Harbor itself was about as barren and desolate a place as could be imagined. Mr. Beatty had had no hand in planning it. No one did; it just grew, like Topsy. A wedge of sandy land between three rocky hills and the harbor, nothing was ever done to improve it, or even make the most of it. The Parry Sound Road circled around the big hill and turned east at the "corner", which was the heart of Parry Harbor, and wound around hills and lakes for 75 miles, until it reached the Railroad.

At the corner were two general stores, one very small, the other well-stocked. A road branched off there to the south for a block, past the company office and our house, and then west to the waterfront, along the shore and lumber yards to the mill. Across from our house to the south was a big plain hotel – a three-storied building then called the Thompson House. At the back facing another road they had a "bar", the nearest one to Parry Sound. We usually did not see much that was going on back there, except on special occasions. When the lumber camps broke up in the spring, and the shantymen, who had been in the bush for months without a chance to spend a penny or let out in any way, arrived in town with pockets full of money, the first thing many of them thought of was to "have a spree". They flocked over to the Thompson House, and most the them stayed right there until their last penny was gone. Then they went to work in the mills.

Behind our house and the office was the stable yard, barns, and stables. It was a large yard with a high board fence around it. We children played ball there and other games when there were no horses in it. We must often have been "under foot", but the stable men were always good natured and thoughtful in a way about us children, but in their joking and laughing with the teamsters their natural vocabulary came out without thought. Between them and the shantymen in springtime we learned quite a few forceful words.

There was a post office, of course, and a school, and a small white Catholic Church on top of a rocky hill with a plain wooden cross on its steeple. The priest, who was either French or Irish, lived at the foot of the hill.

And then the Salvation Army came: Two good-looking lassies from Toronto in neat blue uniforms and Salvation bonnets, a lieutenant, and a captain. They tried unsuccessfully to find a barracks in Parry Sound and had to take an old storehouse in Parry Harbor. It was on the main road, deep sand in front of it to the corner. The day arrived when the barracks was in shape, and they were to hold their first meeting. Soon after supper we heard the drum and the tambourines, and hurried over to the corner. There, coming down the road in a swirl of dust were the captain and the lieutenant beating their tambourines and singing their salvation songs, and beating the big drum was Johnnie Goodneson, who had just come from Iceland with his family and could hardly speak a word of English. He was a big, healthy, good-natured boy about 18 years old, and he beat that drum with enthusiasm. They stopped at the corner, and the captain began to speak. Then they knelt down in the sand and prayed. I couldn't stand it. I rushed home to my room and had a good cry. I guess it scared me to think of what one might be called upon to do if one wanted to be a Christian.

There were some bright spots even in that drab little place. Some really fine people lived there. Nearest to us was Judge McCurry and his family in a pretty house on the hillside overlooking the Harbor. Captain McFarlan and family lived on the hill beyond the Catholic Church in a comfortable, old-fashioned house. They were right from Scotland and raised sheep, while the Captain taught the school. He was a fine looking Scotchman with a nice brogue, and in winter he sometimes wore a plaid. One of their daughters still lives there and is one of our best friends. Mr. and Mrs. James Ellis came soon after we did. They had three daughters, one still living in the old house with their adopted brother, Dr. Oscar Ellis. They were Mother's and Colene's best friends.

J. W. FitzGerald was President of the Company. He built a large fine house on the hill towards town. Later, George Gladman joined the company and built another fine house next to FitzGerald's. Their wives were sisters, and both had large families. Irene FitzGerald and

I were chums. We were the same age and went everywhere together during our "teen age". Irene had everything that I didn't have, like a piano and music lessons, lots of new dresses, and so on. But one time I got ahead of her. My uncle in Detroit sent me a lovely little watch with a fob. Mother had just made me a shepherd's plaid dress. It was shirred from yoke to top of sleeve, and around the hips the same depth, and was an unusually becoming dress. Mother quickly made a small pocket among the shirrs on the left side for my lovely watch, and I wore it somewhere that same day. It was the first watch of its kind in town, and was I popular! Except with Irene who was green with envy. It was not long before she had one, too. In the matter of pretty white pinafores to wear to school over our woollen dresses, I had the advantage. Mother made such pretty ones with lace and embroidery, and Irene had no one to make them for her, so Mother made her two at different times.

There were only four children in our family when we moved to the Harbor: Alex, Colene, Charlotte, and I, but in the next few years four more brothers were added. Jim came first, on the 25th of June, 1883; two and a half years later, Frank was born on December 10; Fritz came along on the 9th of February, 1888; and Ollie was last — St. Valentines Day, 1891.

I was 18 when Oliver Mowat was born. He was named after a man who was Premier of Ontario for 25 years, a liberal, of course, and Dad admired him greatly. Dad came that night and woke me, asking me to stay with Mother while he went for Mrs. Graham, a nurse who had brought all four boys. She was an efficient, kind-hearted woman and one of our best friends. Next morning we found we had another little brother. He was a dear baby and I was very fond of him. The four boys were not at all alike. Their personalities and characteristics went with them all through their lives, true to form, and determined their courses.

Penny Readings

Marooned as we were for six months, we had to depend on ourselves for entertainment. No traveling company, lecturer, or magician came to our out-of-the-way village during those winter months. There were many private gatherings at the different homes in the evening, also Church suppers and concerts, and carnivals at the rink, and then there were "Penny Readings".

A form of entertainment popular in the small villages of England, Penny Readings were adapted to our need. The program consisted of readings, tableaux, farces, short plays, piano solos and duets, songs, choruses, and any kind of an act that was amusing or interesting. Admission was ten cents instead of a penny, and they were held every two weeks in the Music Hall.

The Music Hall was a large wooden structure, useful but not ornamental, with a stage at one end equipped with a drop curtain and wings, and a gallery over the entrance at the other end. A long, cold, dark hall led to the dressing rooms, which were usually warm. Coming out of them into the cold hall and onto the drafty stage, dressed in light clothes and no wraps, of course, it is a wonder we did not catch our deaths of cold, but excitement must have kept us warm, for we were seldom any the worse in the morning. At night, the stage, set attractively with hangings and furniture borrowed wherever they could be found, the owners glad and proud to contribute to the big show, bright footlights, music, and a full house — the old Music Hall appeared quite festive.

Soon after the New Year began, the Captain's daughter came and asked Mother if I could take part in a short musical comedy they were planning for the Penny Readings. Mother approved, and she taught me my song of four lines and took me to the Music Hall for rehearsals. I came on near the end alone, facing for the first time the footlights and an audience. I held a large bouquet of flowers which I presented to Grampa, sang my little song, and then climbed into his arms and went to sleep. When it was over he carried me off the stage "amid loud applause". It was the first of many amateur performances in which I took part extending over years and constituting an important part of my education.

Many of our men and women gave freely of their time and talent, training children and young recruits in their parts for hours at a time, and practicing tirelessly themselves. It brought the whole community together socially, as nothing else could, kept them interested and busy, was educational, and also lots of fun. The Penny Readings were continued for several years, but gradually blossomed out into more pretentious plays, concerts, and comic operas, given three or four times a season.

As the population increased, more and more talent was added to our company of entertainers. Miss Hicock, a teacher of piano and voice, was leader in our musical adventures for years. Two or three times a year, her pupils gave a "Recital" in her drawing room, to which parents and friends were invited. There was usually a tiny musical comedy to relieve the classical atmosphere, some of them so humorous that it was hard to get down to real business at the rehearsals.

In time we gave "Pinafore", of course, and "The Mikado". In these public affairs, all the talent of the town took part. There were weeks of practicing and, as the date drew near, daily rehearsals and a dress rehearsal, which were always discouraging, especially the last, with everyone tired and sure it was going to be a flat failure. But after a day of rest and much coddling by our busy mothers, we would go into it again with renewed zest, and it usually turned out "a great success" — at least the paper said so.

How "good" we were is not the question. It is certain that we were busy and happy, and that we learned a great deal more than we had any idea of at the time. Nor did we appreciate then all that our mothers were doing for us, never complaining of all the costumes — Jap, Gypsy, Scotch, Sailor, Fairy, and numerous others — that had to be made, nor the lack of our help around the home, which was much needed. Tired, but happy, Mother would go with Father to the performance, every word and note of which they had heard many times, not only our own parts but all the other parts, more nervous than we were when we did a bit "solo", and smiling with relief when it was over.

In connection with the Church, we learned all the lovely old hymns and anthems by heart, and became familiar with Oratorios and other sacred music.

Around the piano, we sang Scotch and Irish ballads, popular, patriotic, and university songs, and the newer "rag time" things like "Hot Time in the Old Town Tonight", and the convivial "It's Always Fair Weather When Good Fellows Get Together".

Every public gathering ended with "God Save the Queen", all standing, and not a person leaving until after the last note.

Work and Play

Summers and winters passed much the same outwardly, but each day brought something new and interesting. Several times in summer we went "outside" to visit Grandmothers and Aunties, and they came to visit us, but most of the time we spent at home, not even going on short trips to nearby villages very often.

Our family of boys and girls, each one a personality, brought to the supper table and to our round table afterwards bits of experience and news, and there were problems to be solved and much work to be done.

As the oldest, I shared Mother's responsibility and work, and felt more as she did toward the younger children than as a sister. After graduation from the common school, I stayed home to help her. There was so much sewing to be done, so many button holes to be made, the mending basket never empty, besides the general housework. Mother did most of it. I helped in small ways, but know now that with all my "going" to practices and rehearsals, church work and social outings, that I helped very little and probably made more work than I saved her.

As soon as I was able to read and write intelligently, I became her secretary, writing letters from her dictation and making out the orders to be sent to T. Easton and Company when we had a little extra money to spend. We would all pore over that catalog for hours and when the order was finally made up, we waited impatiently for the parcel to arrive, and when it did come we all gathered round to help open it. Then things were tried on, and the new parlor curtains held up to see if they were all we had hoped. Sometimes there were disappointments and things had to be sent back, but not often. A great deal of this was going on about Christmas time, and then the parcel was brought in stealthily and things put in "good places" to turn over to Santa Claus later.

I stayed up when the younger children were sent to bed, to help dress dolls, or help work on pretty white aprons for the girls to wear as a protection over their warm woollen dresses.

Sometimes I read while Mother worked. I read to her a great deal by the hour, and sometimes by the day when the story was "terribly interesting". When the newspapers came, we read of politics, wars, fashions, and the continued stories together. Father brought home whole sets of Scott and Dickens in paper covers, and I read nearly every one of them, mostly to myself. We loved to read so much, and there was so little time that the stolen opportunities were very sweet. Mother's most precious time was an hour before going to bed, and on Sundays when we did no work of any kind except that of necessity or mercy, and she could spend her leisure reading without qualm of conscience.

Social events were all in the evening in company with our men. We danced a little and played cards a little, though they were more or less frowned upon in private homes. Afternoon bridge parties were unknown and the only woman's club was the "Ladies Aid Society". The ladies paid formal calls in the afternoon and served tea.

The days were fully occupied. There were no "ready-to-wear" stores nor grocery stores filled with canned food. The sewing, including the making of coats and boy's suits, was mostly done at home. The canning also, and much other cooking and baking daily. Rag carpets and rugs, quilts and comforters, and almost everything we used went through the hands of the housewife and her helpers. At home we knitted and crocheted necessary articles of wearing apparel in the evenings, if we did not mend, and when we went to spend the afternoon with a friend, we took our "fancy work" with us. There were few idle moments in a family like ours.

Contact with the "Outside"

Our small community had had telegraphic communications for some time, and now we were to have a telephone exchange. We had read much about the new invention, but many of us had never seen one, and it seemed a wonderful thing that we were to have it in our own town.

When they were installing it in the Company's office, Father came over to the house to tell Mother and me that it was in. He had talked to the operator at Central and could hear him as plainly as though he were in the same room. Father said the operator, who was an old friend, wanted me to come over and talk to him. Father showed me how to use it, and when I had rung the bell and put the transmitter to my ear, I heard a familiar voice calling "Hello." I shouted "Hello," feeling that he could not possibly hear me unless I did. Father said, "You need not shout, just talk naturally," and finally we had a short conversation, but I was eager to rush home and tell Mother all about it.

The railroads were creeping nearer and nearer, shortening the stage trips and making us feel less cut off from the "outside" and greatly increasing travel to and from the city and elsewhere. Toronto was 150 miles to the south. Now they drive up in the afternoon and return to Toronto for dinner. But then there were no autos. Travel was by train and then stage over 75 miles of poor roads.

But now the first boat ceased to be the momentous

event it had been in earlier days. It was still hailed with joy and enthusiasm, as it was our chief supplier for all our needs and a dear reliable friend, as well as a harbinger of open season. But where there had been only a weekly boat, there was now a daily, and several semi-weekly, from South Shore ports and American ports.

Visitors came in greater numbers both summer and winter; talent ventured in sometimes; politicians came to woo us for their candidate; evangelists came to urge us to our duty; millionaire yachts even anchored in our harbor; newspapers and books were plentiful; and we felt ourselves almost at the center of things.

The mills were running to capacity. The river was full of logs, and great rafts of them were in the Harbor for the two mills on its shore. Vessels were loading at the different yards and all seemed to be going well, when word came that our Neighbors had taken the duty off logs and put it on lumber. The natural thing for their lumbermen to do, of course, was to take the logs over to their own mills and saw them there, which they proceeded at once to do. They bought up the logs, and with large tugs towed away the huge rafts, and our prosperity with them.

Gloom settled on the town when they moved away. The weather, as if in sympathy, turned dark and stormy. The wind howled all night, and the waves dashed on the shore.

But by and by a ray of sunshine stole in upon it. Word came of the storm out on the Big-Sea-Water and the fate of the logs trying to cross it: caught out in the open in the full sweep of the wind, the booms were broken and the logs scattered all over the great lake so widely that it would be impossible to gather them together again. It was the last we ever heard of the duty on lumber and, considering how much it meant to the whole community, can you blame us for being thankful?

My First Trip "Outside"

The time came when I was

> "Standing with reluctant feet,
> Where the brook and river meet."

Mother thought I needed a change and a little worldly experience, but how to give it to me was puzzling her. We had gone two or three times during summers to visit Grandmother in The Garden of Ontario for a few short visits, but the rest of the time we had spent at home with few trips even to nearby towns.

The Captains on the lumber vessels had often urged Father to take a trip with them, so when he heard that a party of friends were going down to Detroit on the next trip of one of them, he arranged for me to go also and pay a visit to my uncle who lived there.

There were a few days of intense preparation, and then one beautiful June evening I said goodbye to Mother, my sisters, and brothers, and Father took me and my little trunk in the rowboat across the Harbor to the vessel, piled high with sweet smelling yellow lumber. He took me on board, shook hands with the Captain, thanked him and asked him to see me safely into my uncle's hands. He kissed me and told me to "be good," "have a fine time," "write often," and then he was in the rowboat again and on his way home. I stood at the rail watching him with a lump in my throat and a strong desire to call him back again and ask him to take me home with him.

Before he was out of sight, the ship was on her way toward the setting sun. The water was like a mirror and brilliant with sunset colors. Sitting there on the lumber piles, we watched it disappear, and at almost the same moment the moon came up in the East. The long twilight faded, and the moon then reigned supreme. It was almost as light as day and so calm and peaceful, the only sounds that of the engine and the water purling along the side. The Captain made us more comfortable and we sat there for hours, talking very little except to say once in a while, "It's getting late. We should turn in." Red Rock light came in sight. The Captain said, "It's a long way off," and went to bed. We four thought we would watch until we passed the light, but at 2 a.m. it was still away in the distance, so very sleepily we said "Good night," and went to our staterooms.

In the morning after a fine breakfast, we went on deck again, but stayed in the shade, as the sun was hot and bright with very little breeze.

We passed Cabot's Head Light, where a woman, two children, and some chickens were all the life that we could see. There was not even a tree on that bare rock. They waved, and the salute was returned by waves and three toots of the whistle.

For hours that day we were out of sight of land, so we slept some, read, and ate the good food the cook served, and were ready to enjoy the long lovely evening with its gorgeous sunset and rising moon. The Captain advised us to turn in earlier, as we should be up by 3:30 a.m. if we wished to see the entrance into the river. I wasn't sure I did want to see it at that hour, but knew I should, so reluctantly dragged myself out of my comfortable bed.

The minute I opened the door, all indifference vanished. The moon was still shining brightly, and around us were other boats — dozens of them — all headed in the same direction as we were, converging on the entrance to the river. There were many lights, the boats moved slowly, deep-toned whistles blew, signaling as they came closer together. One at a time they passed in as their turn came. Finally we were in the river. It was broad daylight. On our left was Canada, and on our right the United States of America, which had always seemed more or less of a myth to me. Here it was, actually, and this was the river down which our lumber had been gliding all these years.

So far there had been nothing startling or especially new to me. I loved it all as one does old friends and familiar things. But I was on an adventure and hoped for the new and the wonderful. Surely I would meet people of whose cleverness, charm, culture and beauty I had scarcely dreamed. I hoped to see and hear and feel intensely — to really live.

We passed Grosse Point and Belle Isle and entered the activity of Detroit Harbor. There was a congestion of boats of all kinds and sizes: great grain and ore boats, some of them looking like big brown cigars floating on the water; others carrying freight, passengers, and lumber, all moving majestically southward, stopping at Detroit or passing on into Lake Erie. Crossing their path, the little ferry boats nonchalantly dodged back and forth from the U.S. shore to the Canadian. Small tugs wove in and out, confidently going about their business. Excursion steamers joined the procession with their crowd of pleasure seekers; all along the shore, smaller craft were tied up — and there was the city rearing its massiveness in the background.

Our vessel glided up to the wharf to discharge her passengers. A street led up from the wharf to the city. It was paved with stone. The tall buildings on either side were built of stone, brick, and cement. Not a tree or a blade of grass was in sight, and to my unaccustomed eyes, it looked like a tunnel and a hard proposition. But I was sure it led to beauty, wealth, and wonders unimagined.

I said "Thank you" and "Goodbye" to the Captain and the crew and my fellow passengers, and turned to look up the stony street.

I had a rendezvous with Life. Gaily and confidently, I stepped out to meet it.

Round Trip

Leaving Detroit after a wonderful visit, I crossed the river to Windsor and on to Forest where Aunt Charlotte and Uncle Pete lived. They had a very pretty little home, and Uncle Peter Campbell had a nice bookstore downtown. They both sang in the choir of the Presbyterian Church, and Uncle Pete played a cornet in the band. It was a lovely little Canadian town, and I enjoyed my visit there very much.

Waterloo, Ontario, was my next stop. There in the old homestead I had spent many happy days, and my mind was saturated with the family history and the old town. It was very German. After Grandpa Breimer died and the children went off to homes of their own, Grandma married again, and with her youngest daughter, Sara, went to live in Elmira. The old place was sold, but Aunt Bert and her husband, Will Stirling, still lived in the town, and had a nice home and small family. It was all very interesting, as I had not been there for years, and it was the last time that I saw the old place and those dear people.

From Waterloo I went to Galt to see Grandma and Grandpa Hogg and Aunt Maggie, who was married to Ira Anderson and had three boys, the oldest some years younger than I. Galt is said to be the Scotchest town out of Scotland, and was as different from Waterloo as could be.

Elmira, where Grandma (now Grandma Hollinger) and Aunt Sarah lived, was a small German place, not

135

far from Galt and Waterloo. Aunt Sarah had married Albert K. Dunke, the beau of the town at that time. He was one of a large family living there, and had the "big store". At that time, they lived in an apartment over the store and had two small boys — Harry, about three, and Floyd, one. I stayed there for nearly two months, why I do not know, except that I must have been enjoying myself and time passes on swift wings.

Before I realized it, it was winter, and a determined call came for me to come home immediately. I went to Toronto where I met Mrs. McFarlan and stayed with her at Coverley's overnight. Next morning we took the train for Utterson where we met the stage. All afternoon we slid over the snow-covered roads to the jingling of sleigh bells, and arrived at Rosseau after dark, though it was not yet 6 o'clock. There we had a good supper at the hotel. I was so tired and drowsy as I sat in the warmth of the fire after supper that I could hardly move, but there were still three or four hours of travelling to go, and my dear family was waiting for me.

The team was at the door. They wrapped me up in a fur coat with a blanket around my legs and feet, and over all a big buffalo robe. I sat with the driver and was as snug as a bug in a rug as we went skimming along in the starlit night to the sound of jingle-bells and the squeaking of the snow under the runners.

About midnight the stage stopped at our door, my father disentangled me, and I kissed them all. Oh, how good it was to be home again. When we had all caught our breaths and settled down for a few minutes to talk, the first thing that was said was, "How fat you are!" I weighed 125 pounds and could hardly see out of my eyes — or at least they could not see my eyes. They did not like me so fat, but with all the activities at home and in town, I soon lost it and returned to normal weight which was about 112 pounds.

The Last Year Home

I had one more memorable year with my family in Parry Sound. I didn't know it was the last until it was nearly over. Lex was 18 and a junior clerk in the Bank of Ottawa. We went everywhere together, but never came home together. We went to places of entertainment and parties with our brothers or neighbors, and there we met our special friends and were asked politely if they might walk home with us. It was much simpler under the circumstances and every bit as enjoyable.

It was no small matter for the boys to walk home with Irene and me, as it usually meant a walk of two miles, more or less. That was perfect on a lovely night, but sometimes it was no fun, except being together. One night, for instance, we went to Henry Armstrong's away at the other end of town. It was snowing quite hard when we got there at about 8:00 p.m. We always had a good time at Armstrong's, and thought nothing of the snow. About 2:00 a.m., when we began to think about going home, there was a thick blanket of snow over all the earth — beautiful white snow. There were no autos or taxies, and while everybody had canoes or rowboats, very, very few kept driving horses, so as usual there was nothing to do but WALK. Our young gallants did not hesitate, but went ahead to break a path for Irene and me. Single file we walked all the way home with very little talk. We girls were wet to the knees, and there must have been big business in pants pressing next morning.

We had a nice crowd that last year. Our get-togethers in the past had been irregular and by invitation, mostly. This year we planned to meet regularly at 8:00 p.m. and to start for home not later than midnight. It was more like a club than anything we had had. Every week we did something different, according to the weather, inclination, and opportunity: skating, snowshoeing, tobogganing, coasting. Once we went on a hay ride to a Carling tea meeting.

The evening would end at one of the homes where refreshments would be served. When the weather was unfavorable for outdoor sports, we spent the evening dancing, playing cards or games, or singing around the piano in the dear old "gay '90s" way. Sometimes it was charades. Towards the end of the season we put on a play, which required weeks of study and practice. Irene and I had leading parts in it. Irene was not musical, so this was one of the few times we were in anything together. It was great fun. We performed to a full house and turned in a good amount to a civic project.

The summer passed in the usual way, with many visitors added to our parties, always going in boats and canoes wherever we went. The mills were all running "full blast", many vessels loading at the yards, some full sail vessels with tugs hauling them around. The daily boat between Parry Sound and the South Shore came regularly by way of the south channel, and several semi-weekly, all loaded with freight and passengers, until late in the season.

I was beginning to be a little restless, feeling that I ought to be doing Something Else if I wasn't going to be married. Father had bought 160 acres of land two miles farther down the shore from a Mr. Rose. The prettiest point we called "Rose Point". It attracted the eye of W. F. Thompson, a hotel man, who bought it and built a summer hotel on it. He wondered what to call it, and Dad said, "We call it 'Rose Point'", and Mr. Thompson said, "Good. 'Rose Point' it is," and there it is today on any map of the vicinity, popular with tourists and fishermen.

Dad built a home on the other side of another point, not far from the hotel, which was called "Ettrick" after our one illustrious ancestor, James Hogg, the Ettrick Shepherd. It was a lovely spot in summer, but was hard on Mother and the young folks, as it was so far from all their interests in Parry Sound. I never really lived there and returned only for short visits, so I will leave it to the rest of the family to tell about it.

Canadian girls, up to this time, had not as a rule done anything outside the home except as teachers of some kind or domestics, but now it became quite popular to go into the hospitals and train as nurses. The rules were very strict as to age, education, and character. Several of my friends went to take the training, and it seemed my only outlet.

I had a vague Florence Nightingale idea of a nurse's work, and a very inaccurate one of the reality, so I began to think seriously of it. The age for beginners in Canada was 24, and I was only 20, but one of my friends had been accepted in a Chicago hospital who was just my age. I applied there and was accepted also, on a waiting list, and it was months before the summons came. All this time I was inwardly much excited, one day jubilant, and the next day depressed. When the final telegram came and the day was set, my heart beat so hard and fast that it hurt.

One cold dark morning before daylight in February, 1894, I said goodbye to my dear ones — I don't like to think about it even now — got into the same old stage and rode away on my way to Chicago. The drive was not so long now as the railroad was creeping nearer.

I arrived in Chicago February 13, 1894, and next morning I began this terribly new experience. My old life was over. I was a very bewildered little girl, ignorant of the ways of the world, especially the American world, but by the grace of God and my parents' influence, I came through it unharmed, learned a great deal, and helped a little, I hope.

Not long after my departure, the Grand Trunk Railroad blasted its way through to our point, passing between our place and Rose Point Hotel. Opposite the hotel on our point the station was built and a drawbridge connecting with Parry Island through which our daily passenger boat passed every morning and evening. The railroad went on across the Island to Depot Harbor on its extreme western end, where large elevators were built to store the grain that was brought from the west. The main office was there, and our boys all worked there at times at the beginning of their careers, going over to work on trains or hand cars. Having a railroad so close to one's home is not considered an advantage as a rule, but in this case it was, as it brought life and interest, the telephone, and electric light to our remote spot. Not many trains passed and they always seemed friendly and sociable. The Emma, a large trim yacht, met all passenger trains to accommodate those bound for Parry Sound, which was about two miles by water. Our family had the privilege of going to town on her whenever we wished, which was a very pleasant way of getting there.

There was always a stir at the station in the evening, and our young people would stroll over to watch the daily boat pass through the drawbridge and the life at the hotel, and to visit with their neighbors.

It was really pleasant on a summer's evening and as much fun as anything else.

A few years later the Canadian Pacific Railroad entered the town, passing over the Seguin Valley on a long high bridge to the west side, where their station was built almost in the center of town. All this looked like progress, but now the railroads took over all the business that had been handled by the boats. We were no longer dependent on the boats. The daily boat — "City of Toronto", "Maxwell", "City of Midland", or whichever one it was — continued its trips, but now served mostly the summer resorts, hotels, and campers on its route through the south channel. When the season was over, instead of going on to the end of open season, bravely facing the storms and gales of November to bring us our winter supply, they stopped running and were soon laid up for the winter.

About this time the sustaining industry which had created Parry Sound in the first place finally ran out. The huge timber limits — so huge that it probably seemed that the supply was unlimited -- were slashed and cut regardless of the future. They probably did not understand how it would work out: the effect of clearing the land of all the trees that distribute the moisture and with their leaves fertilize it for another crop. They were greedy, too, to get all the money out of it for themselves that was possible and took no time to consider the result of the ruthlessness. At last there were no more logs to float down the river to the mills, so they stood there idle. The lumber vessels came and carried away the last of the lumber leaving the tramways stark and ugly. The tramways and mills all disappeared finally by fire and demolition, and the water front returned to its original simplicity, except for wharfs and docks, and the water again lapped peacefully on a sandy rocky shore. No more vessels and barges loading at the yards, no whistles and bells regulating the life of the community all summer. The big lake cruisers came into port several times a week, loaded with tourists, often staying long enough for those who wished to go to Calendar to see "The Quints". They are fine big lake steamers crowded with gay tourists that make quite a commotion in town and help to support the community, but after all, they are just pleasure craft, and add very little, if any, to the dignity or real prosperity of a town.

The 20th Century with all its machines and gadgets had its effect on Parry Sound. Streets were paved and brightly lighted with electricity, and automobiles dashed here and there, with a chug-chug here and a toot-toot there. They have a movie theater where all the best pictures are shown, and a golf club, also a library and some new schools. The population is about 3500.

All this is very fine, but old timers like me will miss very much the sleigh bells and the teams of horses dashing through the snow. They seem to be the very spirit of the North. I am glad that the heavens with its sun, moon, stars, and aurora cannot be changed, nor the earth with its rocks and rivers, islands and waterways. If Man were brushed off like the mills were, the earth would in no time return to its own, as though Man had never been, while Earth goes on as vigorous and beautiful as ever.

Chicago

"And I should live a thousand years I never shall forget it." Not because of its greatness, or its goodness, its beauty, or its charm.

In 1894 it was BIG, and it was said to be wicked — very wicked.

Father and Mother warned me, and tried in every way to prepare me to enter it. They knew that there were fine people living there also, and they had great confidence in their daughter.

In the Toronto station, a very fine-looking middle-aged gentleman assisted me with my baggage. I must have looked very small and young, for when I told him I was going to Chicago alone, he stood aghast (the only word that seems to express it), and said, "I have a daughter about your age." I think he said he would rather see her dead, or something equally strong, than to see her go off to Chicago alone.

My uncle in Detroit, with whom I stayed over Sunday, gave me a great deal of advice, and made me promise this and that. I should have been scared stiff with it all, but do not remember any emotion but eagerness to go on, until the conductor came to me as we were entering the Polk Street depot, asking if anyone was to meet me ("No."), and where I kept my money ("In my bag.").

"Put all the money you do not need at once in your stocking, and go straight to the bus over there. If any woman stops you and asks you to go with her, DON'T

GO. Don't talk to anyone but a policeman."

I stepped off that train feeling afraid of everyone but the noble policeman. As I hurried along, someone touched me on the arm. With one glance, I saw it was a woman, and I hurried all the more, but she kept up with asking questions which I did not answer. Then she took hold of my arm and stopped me. I had to look at her, and there on her dress was a white ribbon and on her face a good honest smile. I told her laughingly how scared I had been and why. She walked with me to the bus, told me where to get off and what street car to take. She also spoke to the bus man, and he saw that I got off at the right place.

But my troubles were not over yet. Coming from a small backwoods town, I knew little about streetcars. My destination was on the north side near Lincoln Park, and I had to take a Clark Street car. Many Clark Street cars passed around the Loop, but I couldn't make one stop. Finally I asked a policeman, and he said I was on the wrong corner. He soon had me on the right car telling me and the conductor where I was to get off. Down the street a block or so, I entered a large stone building overlooking Lincoln Park and Lake Michigan, and from the office a smiling young man came forward to greet me. It was the beginning of a new and varied experience which lasted about five years.

I had entered a training school for nurses.

There were many fine hospitals and training schools in Canada. Many of the finest girls in the Dominion had entered them. It was the beginning of young ladies preparing to earn their own living in a profession other than teaching, which up to that time was their only opening except domestic service of some kind. It became quite the fad.

But the age of entering Canadian schools was not less than 24. I was 20, and the time had come when I had to do something. Not being prepared to teach, there seemed to be nothing for me in Parry Sound. Nursing appealed to me, not in the actual doing, but in the opportunity to help suffering humanity, which I had been trained from early childhood to believe was the duty of a Christian.

They were not particular about age in this Chicago school, and I had no difficulty in being accepted as a probationer and in due time as a nurse. I graduated three years later, did private nursing in the city for a year or so, and then went to Waterloo, Iowa, where I met Dad (D.P. Sias), and we were married July 15, 1902.

Nursing still goes on. It is a fine profession, and so necessary. It was a great experience for me, a training that has helped me every day since. Often I wonder what I would have been without it. I met all kinds of people, heard about all kinds of religions and doctrines, was swayed this way and that from my straight Presbyterian path. I was often tempted and often stumbled, but I really wanted to do, and be, right, and as I see it now, never strayed very far.

One thing I noticed — the principles and ideas that I felt positive about before I left home, those my father and mother believed and lived, I never faltered over. They used to say, "You can't budge the Canadian Presbyterian," and one time when I had withstood a siege, one of the men who had been urging me said later, "I am so glad you didn't give in," but he didn't help me with a word.

You young people will all laugh when I say it was only a question of going to the theatre Sunday evening. There were weaknesses. Things Mother had said, things Father had done, things I hadn't quite settled in my own mind that gave me a little leeway, caused me trouble until I learned by sad experience. Like a kid, I took advantage of a little leeway. Mother and Dad did not. They were all right. I understand them now.

When I think of these things I realize what I learned in Chicago. But when I think of Chicago, the memories that come to me are of parks and pictures, music and drama. From my window on the fifth floor, I looked out upon Lincoln Park with Lake Michigan sparkling beyond.

I walked in the park almost daily, sometimes from the north to Lincoln's monument on the south end. I stopped often to feed the animals, wandered through the conservatories, round the flower beds and the lagoons.

My favorite walk was along the lake shore, especially when the old lake was putting on a rampage. The louder the waves roared and the harder they dashed on the seawall, the better I liked it. At night there was often music or the electric fountain, which had been at the World's Fair, and once a month a full moon.

There were other parks and boulevards — even in those days — that I loved, especially Jackson Park, the old fair grounds. We went there in a Hansom cab usually, but sometimes in a carriage and pair. It was a hired carriage, but looked all right and was comfortable until the day of the thunder storm. As we were going through Washington Park, the rain came down in torrents and into the carriage as if the top were a sieve. We were drenched by the time we got to Michigan Avenue where we lived.

Some of the old buildings had been saved from the wreckers, and other attractions, such as Columbus' ships — the Santa Maria, the Pinta, and the Nina — and the Island and its Japanese houses and gardens. The old Ferris wheel had been moved to a beer garden on North Clark Street; I went up in it twice.

On hot summer days, we often drove out there and had our picnic supper near the Gorman building. It was right on the lake shore and comparatively cool, especially in the large building, where I was always fascinated by the big revolving world opposite the entrance. There is one in Miami, Florida, now, in the Pan American Airways terminal, around which there is always a circle of people leaning on the railing, pointing and talking in low tones to each other. So many have put their finger on the spot called Miami that there is a deep worn place as large as the tip of your thumb.

If there were only two of us going, we went in a Hansom cab. If more, in a carriage and pair. We would stay until the sun had gone down and drive leisurely around. By the time we got to the Midway the lights would be on, and a swarm of lighted bicycles, looking like a thousand fireflies, would be gliding up and down the double roadways.

I went often to the Art Institute, and spent hours looking at the pictures. It was a grand place to rest if you were tired and at the same time absorb beauty. But I walked miles around that building, looking at everything it contained, and sometimes watching the art students at work. I did not make a study of it then, but did a little later.

Thurber's, where private exhibits were shown, was another place where I learned to appreciate art, including the art of the "Gay Nineties". Cubist art was just becoming popular, but I never liked it.

I was fortunate in having friends who went often to the theatre, and were generous about taking me with them. If it had not been for these friends I would have seen very little. I did not realize then how much they were giving me. The memory of it all never ceases to give me a thrill of pleasure. It goes through all my life like a golden thread, and bursts out at times in brilliance when I hear some fine orchestra play the same music or read of the celebrities I had the pleasure of seeing and hearing in person. I thank these good friends over and over and wish I could tell them and do something lovely for them, but I do not know even if they are alive. That was 40 years ago.

The first theatre I remember was McVickers. We went in a carriage, and sat in the parquet circle. We were early, and as it was all rather new to me, I was interested in everything and thrilled beyond words, though I probably did not show the half of it — at the people seated around me in the boxes and in the galleries, the curtain with its picture of the World's Fair, and the words "And I should live a thousand years, I never shall forget it."

Then the little doors under the stage opened, and the orchestra, stooping, came through one by one, each carrying his instrument. Then there was the stir of getting seated, placing the music racks and instruments and sheets of music, the drummer with all his paraphernalia, and the tuning of the strings, a moment when all was ready, then the music, sometimes in a burst of sound and sometimes so softly it could hardly be heard.

They played all the lovely old favorites from the operas and other classics, besides all the new good music that came out. I seem to have a good ear for music, for I remember them well. They are still the favorites, played by all the best bands and orchestras, and I enjoy them more and more.

Suddenly the footlights would go on, the house lights would go off, and the curtain would go up, revealing the setting, and so "on with the play."

John Drew was one of the first I saw, with Maude Adams, I think. Lionel, John, and Ethel Barrymore, Maxine Elliot, whom I thought the most beautiful woman I had ever seen, and her sister Gertrude. Nat Goodwin, with his wife Maxine, in An American Citizen, William Gellette in Secret Service and Sherlock Holmes, Richard Mansfield in Cyrano de Bergerac, Ed and Joe Holland, Otis Skinner, Frank Daniels, Francis Wilson, Karla Balue, and others.

Since those days, I have seen very few legitimate plays. Once when Dad and I were in Chicago, we saw The Prisoner of Zenda and another, which I can't remember. In Detroit, years later, we saw Abie's Irish Rose and a few small plays in Orlando, one of which was done by Margaret Angelin.

In New York, we went to the movies. The movies have crowded out real plays to such an extent that there is seldom a chance to see one, and the price, which one paid in the old days without a murmur, seems exorbitant now.

One night at supper, the girls began to talk of cinematograph, which was being shown at the Schuller Theatre as an act in a vaudeville show. They said it was wonderful — it moved. Four of us went down on the streetcar to see it and sat in the gallery. It did not come on until near the last, and we thought we were going to be disappointed, but at last it did come on, and it actually did move. It was a picture of raking leaves by three people who moved about just as natural as could be, and when they set fire to the pile, the smoke curled up. There was a slight shimmer over all the picture, making it look hazy, but it was a marvel to us. One of the theatres was packed — not even standing room. I stood for two hours to see the Stoddard colored pictures and his lecture on Japan. How tame they would seem to us now.

The Thomas Orchestra, 75 pieces, which I heard in the Auditorium, was a great event, and my one Grand Opera, "The Barber of Seville", with Sembrich, which I heard there; also "Herman the Magician".

I loved the church music, but it was not new to me. I didn't think I liked the street music, the music boxes, hand organs, German bands, beer garden orchestras, which we heard all around us, and the calliopes, but now when I think of Chicago, I can hear all these sounds above the street noise, and somehow I like to think of them along with the rest.

There was also the little three-piece orchestra, a harp and two violins, played by three young Greeks, I think. They came around once a week, and the smiling young man who loved to dance always invited them into the hospital for the patients to hear. They played all the popular songs, "Annie Rooney", "A Bicycle Made for Two", and all of that vintage, the Sousa marches, two-steps, and so forth. How lovely it sounded all through that big building, and how we enjoyed dancing to it for that short time. It had to be short, so as not to tire the patients, but as a rule they enjoyed it as much as we did.

I do not remember when I first rode in an automobile, probably in Waterloo, Iowa, in 1901 or '02, but the first one I saw came tearing down Sheridan Road at the rate of 15 or 20 miles per hour. The noise was deafening and the smell awful. It looked like a buggy without shafts going all by itself. "No pushie, no pullie. Go like hellie allie same," as the Chinaman said.

"What is it?" we said.

"Oh, you know. It's one of those things ... "

"What a freak — a plaything for some rich boy. Never be anything more than that." So we said (or thought) in 1899.

I had never heard of one before, but the encyclopedia says, "For its origin we may go back as far as 1770, when Cugnot, a French inventor, built two steam road waggons, and others were constructed in France and England all through the 19th century. The honor of having led in the development of the automobile belongs to France, which explains such terms as chauffeur, garage, chassis, tonneau, limousine, etc." But in the 20th century, no country in the world makes and uses so many beautiful cars as the United States.

From a fourth floor window, I saw [President] McKinley pass down State Street, smiling and bowing with his silk hat in his hand.

Marthine Mathisen, my roommate, and I went to the Stock Exchange. The day before, Leiter had cornered wheat at $1.25. That morning there was great excitement. We sat in the gallery and watched the crowd of men around the different pits, but especially the wheat pit, waving their arms and chewing gum frantically. What it was all about I had only a vague idea, but Chicago history will tell you what really happened.

There were 20 or more telegraph instruments in an enclosure at the side, an operator at each one taking messages simultaneously. How they could get a message straight in all that noise and confusion is still a mystery to me, and the small messenger boys worming their way through the dense crowd and delivering the message to the right man.

I think also of the Gibson Girl with her stiff shirt waist, sailor hat, and long skirt with frilly petticoats underneath. We all looked more or less like her. Dana's pictures were lovely. I gave a book of his sketches as a wedding present, which seemed to make quite a hit.

But the lady who impressed me most, because I was not a bit like her, was the one in a sealskin coat with high collar, or boa, a large hat loaded with ostrich plumes, white kid gloves, calling cards, and a large bunch of fresh fragrant violets fastened to her coat or muff. I have tried to raise violets ever since, but with little success.

The training in the hospital (sanitarium) was a fine thing for me. I remember it mostly for the many things I learned how to do. I was the smallest and the youngest, and was treated accordingly. They were all very nice to me, too indulgent sometimes, so that I fear I never got where all depended on merit, and accordingly was not as good a nurse as I wished to be. But I got along very well, and Dr. Costain used to say, "No one will suffer very much if 'Little Hogg' is around" — a left-handed compliment it seems to me.

I liked them all, but there was no one whom I admired or respected especially, though I met some very clever famous men and women while there.

Christine Thompson, who entered and graduated with me, was a fine girl and I was very fond of her. She went to Knoxville, Tennessee, and later married a doctor, but I have not heard of her since.

The head nurse on the floor where I worked mostly, Marthine Mathison, was really charming in her white uniform and very helpful to me. She was from Bergen, Norway, and came to Chicago when she was about 18. Her manner and foreign accent were charming, her person immaculate always, as though she had just come from the bath. She looked Norwegian with fair, clear complexion, rather light, straight hair, and high cheek bones, but in a very refined and dainty way. She was a good nurse also, and was often sent on very special cases.

At the World's Fair, there was a small perfect hospital. The best nurses from all the different hospitals in the city were chosen for duty there, each one for two weeks, but Mattie stayed for six weeks straight. She had a wonderful time. Men vied with each other for the pleasure of having lunch with her and taking her out in the evening. One, a very fine-looking man connected with the Vose Piano Company of Boston, was the most successful. Almost every night he took her to the best and most expensive theatres, and other places of entertainment.

She had a woman looking after her clothes, making changes in the dresses and wraps daily according to her ideas, and though her dresses were really few, he said she was the best dressed woman he had ever known. When she was too tired to go anywhere, he came with flowers, books, and candy. When I arrived months after, it was still a topic of conversation among the nurses, and I heard all about it. She corresponded with him for two or three years, but, not trusting to her own letter writing ability, she had a clever nurse compose them for her. They were good letters, but he eventually found out that they were not Mattie's, and the end of the story is that he married a rich Boston widow.

When I graduated, Marthine and I took an apartment together, too grand a place for our pocketbooks, where we lived for a year or so. Then she went to Kirksville to take a course in osteopathy. Dr. Still and his son were personal friends, and osteopathy was becoming popular. She married one of their handsome doctors and went to New York to practice. I have heard that they lived very grandly there, with a beautiful apartment, box at the opera, and expensive clothes, and I can imagine that the "Office" would have a hard time keeping up. When I go to New York next, I am going to try and find out what happened to Marthine.

Hospital

The first month or so was hard. I do not remember feeling over-awed or homesick, but I was tired and my feet hurt. A steam-heated building, charged with electricity, was a change from wood stoves and oil lamps. I was so hot indoors and so cold outdoors.

Off duty at night I had to go to my room and attend to my feet, which were blistered and swollen. I bathed them in hot water and applied all sorts of stuff I had never heard of before and was in bed and asleep in no time.

In a few minutes, that heartless night nurse would walk into my room and turn on the light right in my face. "Six o'clock," she would say, and I could have killed her. It was physical torture to try to wake up. But when I had managed it, the thought of the good breakfast and the merry bunch of girls around the table reconciled me, and I could see that it was a lovely morning.

The early ones met on the porch facing Lincoln Park. Across the road was a sheltered sulphur well where bicyclists stopped to rest and drink. Ten or fifteen girls in their pretty uniforms — blue gingham, stiff cuffs and collar, large white apron with a bow at the back, and a white organdy cap with rushing around next to the hair. Every girl was pretty in that uniform, and it was a pleasant sight to see them running over to the well in a flock. They had a good appetite for breakfast and for "duty" at 7:30.

Christine and I were on probation, and we were sent to all sorts of odd assignments that required no experience. Watching insane patients was one that I did not care for. It seemed one of the most awful things to see a human being "out of his head", especially when I had known them when they were or seemed normal. I was not afraid exactly, but very cautious.

One night I put my cot across the doorway, so that the patient could not get by without my knowing it, and fell asleep. A loud crash woke me. The old man was sitting up in bed. He had taken the mug off the washstand and thrown it at me, but happily his aim was not good. It hit the door jamb and broke into a dozen pieces.

There were many funny things that happened, too, and the girls, as they met in the drug room, the diet kitchen, or bathrooms, always had something interesting to relate and many a quiet but hearty laugh about what my old man did or the lady in No. 13.

It was a world in itself. So many people from all over the country, mostly well-to-do, some fine and so interesting, whom we enjoyed and loved to take care of. Others grouchy and complaining, always wanting something else, and it doesn't seem right that those people usually got what they wanted more quickly than the fine ones, just to keep them quiet.

But though we nurses imposed on the good nature of the fine ones sometimes, they had our friendship and received many extra attentions and favors. They got their reward.

Christina and I were soon initiated into the mysteries of the operating room, only as onlookers at first, to see how we could take it. It was rather awful to me, and the first major operation I witnessed I nearly fainted before it was over. Someone noticed how white I was and brought me a glass of cold water, and I was able to stick it out. I couldn't understand the nurses who were present enthusing about it afterwards, calling the operation "beautiful", "perfect", and other superlative adjectives. But soon I was assisting in a minor way and began to understand it and to feel more as they did.

It was an interesting, exciting life, lived mostly within that building. All kinds of people came and went daily. Those who lived there, from the head surgeon to little Annie the dishwasher, were one family. We talked with and gossiped about us all, and when we were sick took care of us. The patients, too, were admitted during their stay, but after they had gone, we seldom saw them again, even those who lived in the city.

We had little time for calling. Every minute of our afternoons off were planned for days ahead, and the distances are so great in a big city that an evening was not long enough. We had to attend lectures almost every evening and to report "in" before 10 o'clock.

Our rooms were on the fifth floor. After the lecture, the day nurses retired, took baths, and put on kimonos. Those who did not go to bed went from one room to the other, talking and playing tricks on each other, or they congregated in one "house" and had a party. Anything was called a party. They were a pleasant, friendly bunch. Now I can't remember a mean one among them or a mean trick.

It seems strange that, much as I liked and enjoyed the men I met in Chicago, not one of them gave me a real "heart throb". I have always liked the company of men, and in Canada had plenty of beaus and dear friends among them, and there was nothing I wanted more than a home, a husband, and kiddies. But I never had a real beau in Chicago, and of course not one I had any thought of marrying. They liked me, and some of them I think were "willing", but it just seemed out of the question.

Thinking it over now, I can see that I had neither "line" nor smart clothes, which was a handicap from the young man's point of view. On the other hand, I was used to outdoor men who could do things — engineers, lumbermen, captains of ships. I loved college men, but saw them only on vacation, when they sailed boats, paddled canoes, walked miles, played tennis, and in the winter, skated for hours, tobogganed and snowshoed, and danced. Several of my best friends became college professors, two of English, one of languages, one of dramatics, or whatever they called it. But I never saw them at work. The men of Chicago seemed pale and artificially sophisticated to me. I respected and admired the work of the doctors, but they were always puttering around in aprons and did nothing besides but play cards, dance a little sometimes, and go to the theatre. They seemed uninterested in literature or the world at large, as a rule. Their ignorance of Canada was appalling to me. Of course, they teased me a lot and probably pretended ignorance often. I liked them all and enjoy the memory of them, but have no regrets.

The Spanish war was going on at that time. Of course, we talked of enlisting, but it was over before we got around to it.

I joined the Fullerton Avenue Presbyterian Church, but went almost as often to the Belden Avenue Episcopal Church, mostly to hear the choir sing. Sometimes we went downtown to hear Gunsaulus or some other notable. We were irregular and often too tired to go anywhere.

[Frank W. Gunsaulus, D.D., L.L.D., 1856-1921,

was a preacher, educator, author, humanitarian, and pastor of the Plymouth Church in Chicago when Wilhelmine Hogg was there. –Ed.]

The first time I went downtown with two of the nurses, I noticed that the people in the streetcar were looking at me, staring really. I finally asked one of the girls, "What is the matter with me? Are my clothes queer? What are they looking at?"

"Your red cheeks," she said.

I had some good and interesting times in Chicago, but I was never really happy there. My thoughts and feelings were a jumble. My beliefs and sentiments had all been challenged and often mildly ridiculed. They were kind and indulgent, but definite in their point of view, and I began to wonder if there was any right or wrong, and good or bad. The sermons were lectures, and I went back feeling that they had little connection with everyday life.

From a charming little Swedenbergen lady I heard that death was a time of rejoicing and a funeral a happy farewell — or should be.

From two fine women living in a lovely home in Highland Park, whose daily lives impressed me so much that I asked about Christian Science, the church they belonged to, I learned about the power of mind over matter, that illness and misfortune were beliefs and did not really exist.

I met Spiritualists, Theosophists, New Thoughters, and read books such as "What all the World's Seeking", "Studies in the Thought World", "The Power of Silence", "The Greatest Thing in the World", "Heaven and Hell", "A Message to Garcia", and many other books, including "Trilby" and all the best sellers.

I forgot to tell about my trip to Parry Sound in 1901. I went by way of St. Paul and Duluth, where I took a boat. I lived on that boat a week and wished I could stay on indefinitely.

The first stop was at Ft. William and Port Arthur. Nothing special happened there, but the air and the scenery made me feel at home and I loved it.

After sailing for a day or two, through a thunderstorm that seemed to surround us, and becoming acquainted with the purcer and the other young people, we stopped at Sault Ste. Marie, where the Stones were living. Maude was at home. Her father was pastor of the Methodist Church. I was with them all day and went to a lacrosse game.

[Pages missing. This next part appears to be about Colene. –Ed.]

. . . training as a nurse. She nursed a little in Waterloo, but having met Florence Ward and her mother, Mrs. Ward, she became interested in kindergarten work. Florence was in charge of kindergarten in Waterloo and a very enthusiastic person, so Colene joined a class under Florence Ward, expecting to make it her work instead of nursing.

But Fate took a hand. I had an urgent call from Dr. Crippen to go to an old patient of mine, Mr. Childs, who had suddenly taken quite ill. I was on another case that I just couldn't leave, so I called up Colene and urged her to go, as I felt we owed it to Dr. Crippen, and I was a little wrong in going on this other case for another doctor.

Colene finally went in my place. Mr. Childs' nephew, Dr. Lyman W. Childs of Cleveland, came to see his uncle, and in about two weeks Mr. Childs died. Dr. Childs returned to Cleveland, but soon wrote to Colene asking more about his uncle's case and for his history sheet. He kept on writing and soon he asked if he could come and see her.

D. Purdy Sias and I had become quite friendly, but I was away so much that he and Colene went out together a lot, as she was home all the time. They used to walk to where I was, sometimes quite a long distance, to see me during that winter. Spring came, and Purdy and I began to think seriously of marrying.

Dr. Childs came, and he and Colene became engaged. That summer, both of us were married, Purdy and I on July 15, 1902, and Colene and Lyman on August 11, 1902.

We expected to be married very simply, but our friends insisted on quite a nice wedding. It was at the home of Mr. and Mrs. Will Newman, where I had been nursing for a month or six weeks. All our friends were there. There were lovely flowers. My wedding dress was of white silk crepe de chene, and I carried a bouquet of sweet peas and lilies of the valley.

It seems hard to write about such personal things, and it sounds queer to me, but we did have as nice a wedding as anyone could wish, and went to a cottage in Cedar Park for the summer.

Colene and Lyman were married at Mrs. Childs' home. Their wedding was much like ours in every way. They went to Parry Sound to see our family, and Lyman liked it so much that they have gone to Parry Sound almost every summer since.

From there they went to Montreal and Quebec and down to Montpelier, Vermont, where Lyman's two little daughters, six and eight years old, were living with their maternal grandmother.

Evelyn and Frances went home to Cleveland with them, so Colene started out with a real family. It has not been easy for her, but she has won out, and her whole family, including her own children, Eleanor, Lyman, Junior, and the twins, Elisabeth and Martha, are devoted to her — and she to them, for she humors them a lot, but gets big returns.

We moved into town, Waterloo, Iowa, at the end of the summer of 1902. Dick was born June 22, 1903, in Ida Ayers house, where we were living. While there, Carlton Sias and his bride, Jeanette Payne Sias, came to Waterloo to live in the same house.

David was then in the wholesale fruit business – the Sias and Cole Company. We built a cottage on Leland Avenue and moved in when Dick was three months old. There we lived until 1905, when the S&C Co. folded up, and we sold the cottage.

An opportunity opened up in Grand Rapids, Michigan, and we went there and lived at 143 Thomas Street, where Ralph was born June 1, 1905, in a small hospital nearby.

In November, 1905, we moved to Sioux City, Iowa, where David went to work for the Orcutt Hardware Company. We lived there until December, 1913.

The big event in Sioux City was the birth of our little girl, Marion, January 8, 1907, in the Samaritan Hospital. We had our two boys, and we were afraid we would have another boy, as so many (at least three) of our friends had three boys and no girls, so I could hardly believe our good luck when the doctor said, "It's a girl!"

There were three Orcutt families besides Father Orcutt, who lived with his son, Merton. They were all perfectly grand to us. We were invited to some of their family parties, which we enjoyed so much.

Florida

I can't remember how we got started on the idea of going to Florida. We began getting the most alluring literature about it, and then David and Merton Orcutt went down one winter — 1911, I think. David bought some land, and from then on our plans were all about Florida.

It was hard to think of pulling up stakes again, but as the wintry winds began to blow, it was pleasant to think of that warm sunny place. We left Sioux City early one December morning. Mr. and Mrs. Merton came down to see us off, good friends that they were. We had said goodbye to all the others, including our friends in the Kindergarten Club.

We spent Christmas with the Childs in Cleveland. After a wonderful week in Cleveland, we had a day in Washington, D.C., our first time there, then took the boat in Baltimore for Jacksonville, Florida. New Year's Day, 1914, we spent in Savannah, and on the morning of January 2, we arrived in Jacksonville, and then in Orlando about 8 pm. In the morning we walked through this beautiful little city and actually saw oranges growing, but none that we could pick.

After a week in Orlando, we got together our equipment for settling on our land, which was ten miles west. It was on a lake that we called Lake Lucy after Grandma Sias.

For a month or more we camped, cooking and eating outdoors and sleeping in a shed built to store

163

things later. Finally our little cottage was finished enough to move in.

And that day, who should appear but Robert Orcutt. Such a surprise! He stayed overnight.

The house was stained brown inside and out. Under a group of young pine trees, fresh and green, the brown house blended beautifully, and seemed to have grown there. It was long and sprawly, and later Ruby Mae called it a little brown "cud of tobacco". It was near the lake shore at the north end and near a bunch of willows, green and fresh in the spring, so we called it "Willow Lodge".

A dock was built out into the lake where we bathed and to dive from.

We had a horse, a cow, and some chickens. We planted five acres of fruit trees, and in between we planted peanuts.

It was three or four miles to Ocoee, where we got our groceries, and two miles to Apopka-Clarcona, and five to Apopka.

We had only one neighbor — the Schermerhorns of Sioux City on the place now owned by the Gibb family.

A mile from us was a real Florida cracker family — the Danns.

We went to church in Orlando, but it took us all day. It was worth it, going once a week to the Presbyterian Church. Soon we had a Ford car, and that was a lot better, but the roads were very narrow (bricked) and deep sand. We never knew when we would get home.

In August, 1914, there was war in Europe. My brother, Ollie, youngest in our family, enlisted in the Canadian Army, and early in 1915 went across with a replacement division of the Princess Pats.

Mother and Dad were alone at Rose Point, and Dad was not well. Mother took care of him all that year. He asked for me and wished I would come. He was always expecting one of us to come, but none of us did, except Colene, who was nearest and went every summer anyway. Mother never told me about that until after he had gone. I would have made a big effort if I had realized, and it is one of my big regrets that I did not go to see my Father at the last. He died in January, 1917. Colene was there, and after the services she took Mother home to Cleveland with her.

In March, 1917, the word was received in Cleveland that Ollie had been killed in action at Viney Ridge. He had hardly had a scratch all that time, but in an instant he was gone. His companion wrote to Mother saying he had not known what struck him, which was one comfort. Mother came to Florida to spend the next winter, and almost every winter after that until she also passed away on April 13, 1935.

Aunt Elva [Elva Hastings, a family friend called "aunt" –Ed.] came first, I think, in 1916 [?], and Uncle Azzie [Azariah Boody Sias, D.P.'s youngest brother –Ed.] in 1915 [?]. Evelyn [Colene's stepdaughter –Ed.] came at Christmas time as she was teaching Spanish in Tampa, and while she was here the telegram came announcing the arrival of twins to the Childs' household on Christmas day. Evelyn was stunned for a moment and then looked up and said, smiling, "I like it."

By this time the U.S.A. was in the war, too. Frank and Fred [Hogg, Wilhelmine's brothers –Ed.] had both enlisted. David [Sias –Ed.]had accepted a suggestion that he go as a Y.M.C.A. man and applied. He sailed from New York in July, 1918.

[Wilhelmine Sias kept diaries about her years at Lake Lucy (the lake is named for D.P.'s mother, Lucy Hebarts Berger Sias) in Orlando, Florida. I have read much of the handwritten pages, sometimes with difficulty but with great interest. There are descriptions of "homesteading" in their hand-built house, their new car, hurricanes, the Great Depression, daughter Marion's marriage, and more. Perhaps someone else will continue Wilhelmine's autobiography by transcribing those diaries and adding them to this book. –Ed.]

Appendix – Autobiography of Colene Childs

[In 2012, as I was working on a new edition of my grandmother's autobiography, I met several "new" cousins by E-mail, all descended from the same great-grandparents, Marie Sophia Breimer Hogg and Francis Ramsay Hogg, through my grandmother's sister, Colene. One of them had received a handed-down copy of my original typewritten and photocopied effort to share my grandmother's autobiography and then found me on the Internet. In 2013, I was sent a scan of Colene's own autobiography, which I transcribe and include here. It appears to have been kept as her journal. I have done the best I can with the handwritten names of people and places. –Ed.]

> Christina Colene (Hogg) Childs
> Born August 4th, 1878
> Parry Sound, Ontario, Canada
> Sunday, 6 a.m.

In a house on the East Side of Church Street, near the corner of Seguin Street.

The family (mother, father, Winnie and Lex) had moved to Parry Sound in May of that year, and father was employed as Shipper for the Parry Sound Lumber Co. Later we moved to the Rogerson Bldg. on James St. (now occupied by the Clark Dry Goods Co.), where Charlotte was born. We also lived for a short period in Dr. Walton's Terrace, overlooking the Seguin River. I have only hazy pictures of those years. About that time father became interested in Manitoba. His brother, James, had located out there and was enthusiastic, and wanted Dad to join him, which he decided to do.

We were all packed and ready to leave, but were delayed on account of a storm and the non-appearance of the boat we were to take. And in the meantime, father received a fine offer from the Midland North Shore Lumber Co. (later Peter's Co.) And our plans were changed, and we moved to Parry Harbor, and lived in the Co.'s house for 15 years, and Jim, Frank, Fred, and Oliver were born there.

That place was home to me, where I grew from childhood to young womanhood, and experienced the things that made up the life of a normal Canadian girl in the 'nineties. I attended the Central School, which meant a 3-mile walk daily, in all kinds of weather. We carried our lunches. Charlotte and the boys went to the Harbor School.

The hotel nearby was operated by W. F. Thomson (now Kipling Ho', a less imposing building. Mr. Thomson later became the owner of Rose Point Hotel.) It was mostly patronized by people connected with the lumbering business, and when the men came in from the camps in the spring, they proceeded to make things lively and spend all their hard-earned money. Of course, we were not averse to viewing any excitement, and there was plenty of it. Once a week they would hold square dances in the big dining room, and we children would climb up on the rocks and watch the performances.

From the company we were able to get a large

supply of blocks — different sizes in kindling wood to be used during the winter. In the meantime the boys would build houses with them, and they were very clever, and it was always a sad time when our playhouses had to be pulled down.

There was a big rock in the center of the field back of our house, and we used it for all kinds of "plays".

Down near the Bay lived an Icelander family; the father was a Shoe repairer. We loved to visit them, and always rec'd some rock candy, which was always on hand. They were nice friendly folks.

Then bordering on the street was the office of the Midland North Shore Lumber Co. (where father worked) and where all the executives gathered, and there was always something interesting going on there.

There was a great deal of business activity in Parry Harbor at that time, and we had a congenial group of families located near us (Fitzgeralds, Gladmans, Mc-Currys, Elles, Pierce, Rosses, etc.), but our school, church, and social activities were centered in the west ward, and we thought nothing of traveling to and from, and on foot, our only transportation. We were all expected to attend Church and S. Sch. And preparations called for the Sat. night bath, shoes polished, and clothes laid out. I realize now the work for mother to outfit her large family on a limited income and all. Our clothes were hand sewn, and we were always neat and clean.

The house was painted white and had green shutters (blinds) at all the windows and on two double doors leading to the lower and upper verandahs, and they were for use. I can still feel the coolness and restfulness of our rooms on hot days when the blinds were adjusted to keep out the glare of the sun.

The verandahs (porches) added greatly to the attractiveness and enjoyment of our house. They faced the west overlooking the Bay, and from there we could view the Harbor life. Boats coming and going, tugs pulling huge booms of logs, lumber barges (consorts) with their sailing vessels in tow, tying up at the different lumber yards to be loaded, and sail boats, row boats — always something doing to claim your interest.

From the upper porch we used to watch for the appearance of the "Northern Belle" (a tri-weekly event) behind Bob's Island. First her mast would be visible, then a trail of smoke and a whistle as she rounded Three-mile Point. From the South Channel, the "F.B. Maxwell", a side-wheeler, made daily trips between P[?] and Parry Sound.

The boats carried practically all the freight, as our nearest railroad connection was 50 miles away at [?]tterson, and they ran a daily stage to that point over a very rough road. In winter, roads were good.

Supplies were low in the spring, and the advent of the first boat was eagerly awaited, and everyone turned out to greet it. The boats were loaded to the limit, decks and all. One of Father's duties was to look after the Store House at the dock at the Harbor, which was a busy place when the boats unloaded. We used to go down often to watch the activities.

I left home February 17th, 1897, a cold, stormy day, enroute to Elseuir Out, to visit Aunt Sarah and Uncle Albert. They had gone through a terrible experience the a.m. after Christmas, when their oldest son, Harry, 6 yrs., was fatally burned while attempting to light the candles on the tree. The shock left Auntie in a nervous condition, and Uncle asked me to stay with them for awhile. They were wonderful to me, and I hope I was a comfort to them. I enjoyed the town life and made many friends.

Carl was born August 13, 1897.

I took a trip to Seaforth, on the Queen's birthday, 24th May, to see Aunt Carrie and family.

Lex paid us a visit on his way to Chicago, Jan. 3rd, 1898, and also stayed with us when he returned April 3rd.

A year and three months passed before I left there, and instead of returning home, I proceeded to satisfy an urge to see the world, and the available outlet was the Jackson San [Sanitarium], Dansville, N.Y., and May 21st, 1898, I started for my new location. The evening before I left, my friends had a surprise party for me and I received lovely volumes of Shakespeare and Scott. The trip seemed complicated, as I had to change Depots in Buffalo, and the confusion and bustle awed me. I arrived at Dansville Station (a mile from town) 7:30 p.m., and it was getting dark and raining. The bus (I should have taken the Sanitarium bus) deposited me at the foot of a steep hill, and I was informed that the San was "up the path", but I could see nothing but woods. By that time I was so lonely and homesick that I would have given up everything to be back in Canada again, and that feeling continued for many weeks. Homesickness is very real and distressing from one who knows.

I walked up and up the hill, and all at once the large Sanitarium Bldg, ablaze with light, appeared. It fairly took my breath away, it was so big and beautiful. A Parry Sound friend, Miss Eva Armstrong, who influenced me to go there, met me at the entrance, and she helped me through the difficult period of adjustment. At that time there was considerable resentment against Canadian girls in the U.S., especially nurses, and there was some friction among the groups there, but I got along nicely, and was apparently successful, as I was given many special assignments.

I spent a quiet but busy year in Dansville. Institution life was new to me, but I enjoyed it very much and visited Buffalo and Niagara Falls (first time) July 1-3, 1899, with Elizabeth Babcock and Ida McPerson. We were thrilled with everything, but my pleasure was somewhat marred, as I lost my pocketbook with ticket and money, and had to borrow from the girls and purchase a ticket back.

I went shopping in Rochester, N.Y., July 29th, and bought a suit and accessories. I started for home on my vacation, August 31st, 1899, going to Lewiston and boat to Toronto, where I stayed all night at the Y.W.C.A. on Elm Street.

It rained next morning, and I got wet going to the train. I was so excited all day as I was nearing home.

I met Mr. FitzGerald and Mr. Lee on the boat going up from Passetang. I will never forget the happiness I experienced when we landed at Rose Point, and I saw my family again. Winnie was home from Iowa, and we were reunited once more. I had not seen her for five years, and we had a lot to talk over. She returned to Iowa ten days later. I noticed a great change in the little boys and Lottie, but more so in Jim. He seemed a stranger to me.

Mother and Lex looked natural, but father had aged. Lottie and I had a good time visiting, exploring Depot Harbor, and seeing friends in town. I was not going to allow Mother to do any sewing for me, but before I left, I had a new supply of clothes. Dear Mother; her every thought was for her children, and I wonder if we can ever repay her.

I left home again October 22nd, 1899, in company with Ella Reatty. It was hard saying good bye. Ollie said, "Why can't we all live together?" and I wish we could. I never appreciated my brothers as I do now. Lex, Jim, Frank, Fred, and Oliver.

Ella and I had an interesting trip. Mr. McQuade told us to go via Midland and connect with our train in Orillia to avoid the long wait at Passetang. We did so, but unfortunately missed our train, and had to take a different route to Toronto. We went to the Walker House and stayed all night.

Next afternoon, I took the train for Elvira, and received a surprise when Sir Wilfred Laurier and party entered our car and took the double seat directly opposite me, and I had the pleasure of listening informally to Canada's silver-tongued orator.

I had a nice time with Auntie, Uncle, and old friends. Expected to leave November 1st, but work at the Sanitarium was dull, so I had to await a call.

Then came a letter from Mrs. Margaret Bottome (from the San) asking me to accompany her to New York, and I was all ready to start when a second letter arrived saying that she had reconsidered and that expense too great. It was a disappointment, for I was anxious to got back to work.

Finally Dr. Gregory sent for me, and I returned to the Sanitarium December 13th, 1899, and went on duty next morning. We had a nice Christmas that year. I was given a lovely yellow silk petticoat from Paris from Miss Palmer and the girls at 18 Aurora Cottage. I thought it was the most beautiful garment I had ever seen. In January, Mrs. Bottome came to Dansville, and when she found I was there, renewed the offer. Arrangements were made with Miss Palmer and Dr. Gregory, and in less than a week, I found myself in the big city of New York. We took a Sleeper enroute, my first experience.

Mrs. B. lived in an apartment at 244 East 13th Street with her youngest son, a lawyer. I was enthusiastic for a while, as I was thrilled with the city and its life and bustle, but I did not enjoy the set-up, and after a month decided to leave. I put in an application at the Employment Bureau at the Y.W.C.A., and the same day I left Mrs. B. – February 20th, 1900.

I secured work in Newark, N.J., and at 4 p.m. arrived at 574 High Street. My patient, Mrs. William Ryerson, was very ill with spinal meningitis, and I was there many weeks. Fortune favored me when I entered that family, for they were so helpful and friendly, and through Dr. Fensmith, their physician, I was given plenty of work and made some nice contacts.

My next case was in S. Orange, 175 Turrell Road, taking care of two small boys, Edwin and Warren Stewart.

Next, Miss FinGado, sister of Mrs. Lee, 44 New Street, very low with typhoid fever. We had a trying siege with her, but she recovered.

Mrs. Lee kept boarders, and as I wanted someplace and liked the folks assembled there, I decided to make that my headquarters. A Miss Condit, one of the guests, was very good to me, and whenever I was at liberty, we would go on trips to interesting points – the beaches on Staten Island, Glen Island, up the East River, Statue of Liberty, and every worthwhile spot in New York City.

June 8th, 1900, I went to 96 Washington Street to take care of two children who had whooping cough. The Polhelmens family was outstanding. They were of Dutch ancestry, and they had refinement and money, but with it all, a simplicity and sincere friendliness that was ideal.

In July, I went with them to Stamford, a small town in the Catskill Mountains, and was there three weeks. I loved the mountains and the trip up the Hudson.

Some more patients:

A Miss Hayes, 288 High Street, widow of a judge. A case of nerves and a peculiar woman.

Rev. Hannibal Goodwin, 116 Mountclair Avenue, an inventor of Kodak film. Broken leg. A character. His daughter remarked, "Miss Hogg, don't ever marry an inventor."

February 21, 1901. Over four months have passed since I last wrote in this book, and many things have happened in that short space of time. I expected to remain in Newark for some time, and here I am in Waterloo, Iowa, hundreds of miles from New Jersey. I cannot realize it yet. Wilhelmine wrote, suggesting that I come out here and live with her, assuring me of plenty of work. So I decided to go west and here I am, and glad of it. It is so pleasant to be with her, although sometimes weeks pass, and we do not see one another. We have two good-sized rooms at E.L. Johnson's, a banker, on 334 Commercial Street, and are very comfortable, and we get our meals, when off duty, at Mrs. Williams, two doors away.

But to return to Newark, October, 1900. My last patient was a Mrs. Ward, who was ill at her friend's home, Mrs. Knevitt, 173 Midland Avenue, Glen Ridge. After a week, she was taken to the Mountain Side Hospital, Montclair. I rode the four miles with her in an ambulance, a new experience. She was operated on by Dr. Ill [Illick?], for cancerous tumor. I was her night nurse for six weeks. She recovered from the operation, but she was a difficult patient, and fought against everything and everybody, and finally passed on November 29, 1900.

The nurses and Miss Illick were so kind to me, and they wanted me to enter the hospital, but the letter from Iowa had been received and my plans made. I was sorry to say goodbye to my Newark friends, for they were very loyal. I had Sunday dinner at the Polhelmens. Mr. and Mrs. Ryerson gave me their blessing, and they thought I was doing the right thing.

I left Newark, N. J., Monday evening, 6:25, Penn. R.R., December 14, 1900. Mr. and Mrs. Lee, Marjory, Miss FinGado, and Miss Condit went to the Depot with me. Trip pleasant, uneventful. I reached Waterloo, Iowa, Wednesday, 8:00 a.m.

Wilhelmine was there to meet me, and I was so happy. It was very cold, and I recall how Jack Frost nipped our ears when we crossed the bridge to the west side. We went to Williams, for breakfast, and I was introduced to the friends. They were all interested in the "little sister". Mrs. Ward and Florence (the kindergarten supervisor), Miss Taylor, Mrs. Girton, Mr. Liffering (lawyer), D.P. Sias, Miss Ballou (teacher), and so on. Later we went to our rooms, 400 Commercial Street, and visited for hours.

At 5:00 p.m., Wilhelmine received a telephone call from Cedar Falls, seven miles, asking her to take a case. She did not want to refuse, but she was taking care of Baby Cassaden nights, and she suggested my going. Of course, I was not anxious to go, but I needed the money, so I consented, and left early next a.m.

My patient, a Miss Johnson, heart trouble, Dr. Peebles in charge. I stayed there two weeks, leaving Christmas Day to go on a case, 3 1/2 miles from Cedar Falls.

Christmas morning I went down to Waterloo for a few hours' visit with Wilhelmine. We exchanged gifts, opened the home parcels, discussed the news, and ate dinner together, and then I had to hurry away.

When I returned to Cedar Falls, Dr. Hansen was waiting for me, to drive me out to my patient. A boy, 13 years, sick with typhoid fever. It was a hard and a worrisome four weeks, and I was lonesome, and I was glad to get back to Waterloo, but I was only there a few hours when I was called back to Cedar Falls. This time my patient was a Mrs. Harrison. They had a beautiful home, work easy, and I was there one week.

February 9th, 1903. Two years later.

I am sorry I did not continue this writing while I was in Waterloo. I have just re-read these pages, and have enjoyed doing so. Some of my experiences were hard to go through with at the time, but they were a help, and I needed the lessons, and the bright spots in my life more than counter-balanced the unpleasant ones.

Name Index

Hogg

James, b. 1770 – Selkirkshire, Scotland (known as "The Ettrick Shepherd", probably a relative), 4, 6, 7, 10, 19, 139

Francis, b. 179? – Selkirkshire, Scotland. Wilhelmine's great-grandfather, 6–8, 9, 20, 23.
Children: James, George "Uncle Geordie", 9–11.

James, b. 1815 – Scotland. Wilhelmine's "Grandfather Jamie", 10, 11, 14, 52.
Children: Christine, Francis "Frank", Maggie, James, Archibald, Charlotte, Edward, 11–12.

Francis (Frank), b. 1845, Galt, Ontario Canada. m. 1870 d. 1917, Parry Sound, Ont. Wilhelmine's father, 11–12, 31–37, 164.

Frederick Archibald, Wilhelmine's paternal uncle, 12, 48.

Charlotte, Wilhelmine's paternal aunt, 12.

Christine, Wilhelmine's paternal aunt, 11.

Edward, Wilhelmine's paternal uncle, 12.

James, Wilhelmine's paternal uncle, 9–12.

Maggie, Wilhelmine's paternal aunt, 12.

178

Hogg (continued)

Breimer

Breimer (continued)

William, Mother's brother, 27.

Henry, Jr., Mother's brother, 27.

Carrie, d. 193?, mother's sister, "Aunt Carrie", 29.

Bertha, Mother's sister, "Aunt Bert", 27.

Sarah, Mother's sister, "Aunt Sarah", 27.

Ramsay

Barbara, b. 1810 Scotland d. 1864 Wilhelmine's grand-mother, 10, 14–15.

James, Wilhelmine's second cousin, 16.

Jean, Wilhelmine's great aunt, 16.

Norman, Wilhelmine's great-uncle, 16.

Index

Index

Index

Parry, Sir William Edward, 54
Penny Readings, 122–124

R

Ramsay
    Barbara, 31
    Barbara (Wilhelmine's grand-
        mother), 10, 14–16
    James (Wilhelmine's second
        cousin), 17
    Jean (Wilhelmine's great
        aunt), 16
    Norman (Wilhelmine's great-
        uncle), 16
Robinson, Mrs. Wallace, 29
Rose Point, 22, 42, 138, 139, 164,
    172
Rose Point Hotel, 140, 168
Royal Canadian Air Force, 40
Royal Navy, 54

S

school, 22, 23, 29, 31, 59, 67, 70, 84,
    85, 92, 101, 103, 109, 168
Scottish Chiefs, The, 32
Seguin River, 57, 168
Shade, Absalom, 18
Shade's Mills, 19, 20
Shenique, Father, 51
Sias and Cole Company, 162
Sias, Azariah Boody, 165
Sias, Carlton, 162
Sias, David Purdy, 145, 161–165,
    176
Sias, Jeanette Payne, 162
Sias, Lucy Hebarts Berger, 165
Sias, Wilhelmine Ramsay Hogg, 3
Sioux City, Iowa, 44, 46, 48, 49, 162–
    164
Skene, Captain, 75, 76
Starkey, Arthur, 77
Steadman, Phillip, 18
Still, Dr., 153
Stirling, Will, 135

V

Van Chultus, "Inchie", 29
vaudeville, 149
Vermont, 41, 161

W

Walton, Dr., 115

Waterloo, Iowa, 41, 145, 150, 160,
    162, 175, 176
Waterloo, Ontario, 9, 25–30, 35, 51,
    52, 135, 136
Waubuno, 53, 62, 90

Y

Yoccasippi (Cargill), 39, 51
Young, Mr., 6, 10

183

www.ingramcontent.com/pod-product-compliance
Lightning Source LLC
Chambersburg PA
CBHW031317040426

42443CB00005B/113